Environment and Fiction

Özden Sözalan / Inci Bilgin Tekin (Eds.)

Environment and Fiction

Critical Readings

PETER LANG

**Bibliographic Information published by the
Deutsche Nationalbibliothek**
The Deutsche Nationalbibliothek lists this publication in the Deutsche
Nationalbibliografie; detailed bibliographic data is available online at
http://dnb.d-nb.de.

Library of Congress Cataloging-in-Publication Data
A CIP catalog record for this book has been applied for at the
Library of Congress.

Printed by CPI books GmbH, Leck

ISBN 978-3-631-81981-4 (Print)
E-ISBN 978-3-631-83415-2 (E-PDF)
E-ISBN 978-3-631-83416-9 (EPUB)
E-ISBN 978-3-631-83417-6 (MOBI)
DOI 10.3726/b17530

© Peter Lang GmbH
Internationaler Verlag der Wissenschaften
Berlin 2020
All rights reserved.

Peter Lang – Berlin · Bern · Bruxelles · New York · Oxford · Warszawa · Wien

This publication has been peer reviewed.

www.peterlang.com

Table of Contents

Özden Sözalan

Introduction

"Human", "nature", and "environment" continue to occupy their privileged place among the inexhaustible themes in literary and cultural
representations. Verbal or visual, most representations are, after all, about
human beings and their relation to the physical and social environment. As
environmental crises grow increasingly more threatening for human and
non-human life on our planet, the need to ask new questions pertaining
to the ways we think about the interconnections between those concepts
becomes pressuring. The latest pandemic has reminded us once again,
that "people are entangled in co-constitutive relationships with nature
and the environment, with other animals and organisms, with medicine
and technology, with science and epistemic politics."[1] To think of a virus
originating in an animal body that can infect millions of human beings
simply because it is capable of traversing corporeal boundaries between
the human and the non-human animal. Not only that. The resulting global
scare has already led to huge changes in our habitual ways of working,
producing, studying, making art, socializing, and travelling. These seem to
be indicative of a shift of paradigm in "culture", too, the domain we once
took to be solely of our own wilful making. As much as human interference in nature and the environment has been causing colossal damage on
a global scale in our age of the Anthropocene, thus changing it irrevers-
ibly, our cultures are simultaneously being transformed according to the
mandates of natural and non-human phenomena. So, yes; we are "fully
in nature," in the same sense as "nature is fully in us."[2] Therefore, the
theoretical re-positioning of the human subject vis a vis nature begs for
radical changes in our conceptualizations of once all-too-familiar terms,
too. Instead of the conventional understanding of human positioned in

---

1 Cecilia Asberg and Rosi Braidotti, "Feminist Posthumanities: An Introduction",
   A Feminist Companion to the Posthumanities, Springer, 2018. 1.
2 Cecilia Asberg and Rosi Braidotti, "Feminist Posthumanities: An Introduction",
   A Feminist Companion to the Posthumanities, Springer, 2018. 1.

an oppositional relation to nature in compliance with the modern divide between culture and nature, we are beginning to think of ourselves not only in relation to environment but as always already environed embodiments, impacting on as well as impacted upon by natureculture.

Works of fiction depict imagined worlds which may closely or remotely resemble the one we inhabit. With the help of specific formal and stylistic devices and depending on the manner of representation, those imagined worlds are indeed commentaries cast on the way we lead our material and spiritual lives. Therefore, representation matters. For the symbolic categories we use to refer to things condition the ways we know about ourselves and relate to our environment. In other words, our perceptions of life, human and non-human alike, are fashioned by the images and perspectives provided by linguistic and aesthetics systems of representation. Yet we tend to ignore the fact that our convictions and judgments are determined by the specific forms through which we speak and see, and that even our interactions with nature are tainted by those filtering systems. Literature and art matter because, while depending heavily on, and contributing to the reproduction of, such symbolic categories in order to mean at all, they also have at their disposal the privileged tools with which to question, challenge, and disrupt those categories. Literary and artistic works keep drawing attention to the artifice of the words and images used in everyday communication – the stereotypical images of the "happy family" in commercials, for example – as well as the very apparatuses and conventions of the medium – the devices of framing, and perspective mainly serve to "naturalize" the power relations and acts of injustice concealed in/by verbal and visual constructs. Art's subversive potential lies in its ability to expose the framing devices inherent in any representation; good art makes us aware of the identificatory and perspectival processes involved in our modes of thought and action.

Nature as origin or as inspiration has always been a favorite resource for literature and art. Under current ecological threats, contemporary fiction's take on nature seems to be engaged with environmental issues in ways that are remarkably more committed and creative than ever. Literary and cultural criticism has, on its part, responded with vigor. Profoundly ground-breaking theories which had already begun to flourish in the field of literary and cultural studies in the latter part of the 20th century continue to provide us today with innovative strategies of reading. Informed by interdisciplinary environmental studies and theories of posthumanism, new critical methods enable us to approach new texts with new tools as well as allowing us to re-interpret texts from the past with new insight. Our growing awareness of the complexity of the relationships we have with nature and the environment, with non-human animals and organisms as well as with science and technology require that we refigure our own relational positions as readers and spectators, too. To understand and to account for the ways in which works of representation reinforce or challenge the anthropocentric system of thought responsible for the creation of hierarchies and antagonisms rather than foregrounding interconnections and interdependencies, it becomes imperative that we broaden the scope of our critical questions to embrace this new awareness: What are the forms by means of which a certain view of life, of nature, and of the human is reproduced and perpetuated in literature, in film or in the theater? How do nature documentaries construct the species? Which assumptions about the centrality of the human are implicitly suggested in films about "man's struggle against nature" or in novels about "man's relationship with animals"? How is oppression normalized through structures of language used in novels associating the Other with the natural? How is the divide between nature and culture deconstructed in contemporary poetry? Which new manifestations of the posthuman are visible in art works and products of popular culture? What kind of new forms are likely to rise that are better suited to express current structures of feeling underscoring our anthropocentric age?

The essays in this volume engage with these questions, in their various articulations, and offer critical readings that display the theoretical diversity in the current reconsiderations of the place of human in relation to nature and the environment. Written by scholars working in separate yet closely related disciplines in the field of humanities, the essays present analyzes of literary and cultural texts, performed with the critical tools provided by studies in ecology, ecofeminism, urban studies, posthumanism and animal studies as well as genre-specific approaches. Some essays in this volume re-visit familiar texts with a view to tracing in them the symptoms of our deep-rooted anthropocentric assumptions while others look at new texts to see the ways in which they articulate new possibilities for envisioning a better world. Any text can be the subject of critical inquiry regarding the role of representation in the human relationship with the environment. Therefore, the forms and genres of texts discussed in the essays are diverse; they include novels, short stories, poems as well as narrative and documentary films, dramatic plays and theatrical performances. Likewise, geographical, temporal and language limits that are used, albeit often arbitrarily, to demarcate the scope of our academic studies become redundant when texts are subjected to an environment-oriented reading. Our increasingly growing awareness of our always already environed earthly existence requires that we develop even more innovative ways of thinking in non-anthropocentric and non-dichotomic terms that seek interconnections and alliances across boundaries. This volume hopes to represent an instance of such diversity.

The first essay in the volume, **The Urban Body in Edgar Allan Poe's "The Man of the Crowd"**, takes us on a tour of 19th century London, a setting spatially and temporally synonymous with industrialization, modernization, and urbanization. Sinem Yazıcıoğlu argues that in Poe's short story "A Man of the Crowd", the bourgeoning city and the emerging urban subject inextricably shape, and are inscribed on, one another in the new paradigm marked by the modern divide between nature and culture. Her reading historicizes Poe's text to reveal the links between the modern construct "city" and its repressed others including first and foremost nature itself, and linking nature and the natural with the lower classes. Concentrating on the relation between the human body and the metropolis in the text, she refers to the ideas of city planning which use the human image as model and the British and American discourse on urbanization to analyze the narrator's examination of the city through the faces in the crowd and his fixation on a particular man. As human interference exacts its toll on the environment, the city is shown to be moulding its own categories of the human subject. The man in the crowd embodies the city itself, as Poe's use of a descent-and-return narrative and the doppelgänger in the context of urban environment is shown to be relating the troubles of urbanization to the form of the human body.

İnci Bilgin Tekin's discussion of two dramatic texts expressive of the disastrous consequences of the capitalistic exploitation of nature involves, too, the interconnectedness of bodies and habitats, albeit on a different plane. **An Old Debate, New Perspectives** offers a comparative reading of Caryl Churchill's *The Skriker* and Cherrie Moraga's *Heroes and Saints* which highlights the fact that it is the most vulnerable of the earth who greatly suffer the consequences of environmental troubles. A timely consideration for the current global crisis we have been experiencing as the casualty and unemployment statistics on the latest "natural" disaster has brought the economic and social inequalities back on the agenda. Born as a head due to excessive use of pesticides, Cherrie Moraga's heroine, Cerezita, in *Heroes and Saints* serves as a metaphor for poor Chicana children dying of cancer and babies born with disabilities in real life California. Similarly, in Caryl Churchill's *The Skriker* the titular protagonist, a shape-shifter drawing on British folklore, who warns of an "unprecedented catastrophe" awaiting "the world as we know it" challenges familiar assumptions about a humanity gone wrong as the planet itself appears at the brink of extinction. Tekin argues that in both plays the dramatization of the exploits of mythological figures in modern contexts is a choice informed by ecofeminism in its insistence to draw attention to the links between the anthropocene and the capitalocene.

Examining the human induced regimes on the environment through literature and film may give way to reconsider the socio-cultural dynamics that shape the Anthropocene age and the possibility of achieving a holistic approach at a broader scale. The political and cultural dynamics shaping the Anthropocene are further examined in the next essay, **Embodied Anthropocentrism in Anatolian Novel and Film,** on Necati Cumalı's novel *Susuz Yaz (Dry Summer)* and its film adaptation by Metin Erksan, the winner of Golden Bear at the 1964 Berlin Film Festival. Ekin Gündüz Özdemirci and Nilay Kaya focus on the ways these narratives question "nature as property" and defend "the right to water" within discussions on environmental ethics. They examine the ecological understandings in both literary and visual narratives, and how they reflect the embodied anthropocentrism that continue to shape the rural and urban environments in modern Turkey, illustrative as well of the global manipulation of water resources in the form of dams, reservoirs or canals due to an instrumentalization of the natural environment reduced to resources that can be easily exploited and consumed.

That anthropocentrism is ultimately a "political" regimen bent towards the destruction of all life forms is further explored in Burcu Kayışcı Akkoyun's essay on Zülfü Livaneli's *Son Ada (The Last Island)*. Burcu Kayışcı Akkoyun's **Intersections, Interventions, and Utopian Pessimism in Son Ada (The Last Island)** examines Livaneli's 2008 novel which portrays the short-sighted policies of a manipulative authoritarian figure, and the ensuing catastrophic transformation of a fictional island from a *eutopia* into a dystopia. Analyzing Livaneli's intersectional critique of authoritarian and anthropocentric perceptions through what she calls an "environmental chronotope," Akkoyunlu argues that the novel's significance lies in the author's endeavor to transcend not only the generic labels and national boundaries but also the binary formulation of culture and nature, which operates to the detriment of both human and non-human "Others." Her reading is mainly informed by Val Plumwood's formulation of "hegemonic centrism" and focuses on the interconnectedness between individuals and species as well as the implications of authority, evil, consent, and solidarity.

Ayşe Beyza Artukarslan in **The Cat, the Cock, the Maid and Zeberjet: The Animals of Motherland Hotel** examines another Turkish novel with focus on its central character's relation to human and non-human animals: the maid, the hotel's black cat, and the gamecocks. In Yusuf Atılgan's celebrated novel *Motherland Hotel* the protagonist Zeberjet stands as an allegory of the human subject faced with his humanity; Having shut himself in absolute loneliness, Zeberjet sees everyone and everything that do not resemble himself as an object, calling into question a Kantian ethics, underlined by the struggle of not losing one's humanity and not resembling non-human animals. Moving beyond the traditional anthropocentric interpretations of the novel, Artukarslan's view of Zeberjet as a critique of the state of the "human" points to the narrative representation of the human as the species responsible for the current ecological crisis in light of the contemporary understanding of the symbiotic relationships between human and non-human animals.

The conventional documentaries "recording" non-human animal life easily conceal the human intrusion involved in the process of their production because the claim to unmediated representation can be made even more boldly with films "reflecting" nature. The framing and narrative devices of the documentary form enabling the illusion of reality are, in fact, comparable to those involved in any fictional representation claiming to hold a mirror to real life. Zeynep Talay Turner's critique of Werner Herzog's *Grizzly Man* entails a discussion of "documentary", providing a meticulous close reading of the representational tools of a genre which is otherwise unquestioningly taken to mirror "truth" and "reality". In *Grizzly Man:* **From the Ethics of Film to the Ethics of the Animal-Other** Turner focuses on Herzog's 2003 documentary about the amateur environmentalist-activist Timothy Treadwell who spent a considerable amount of time with grizzly bears in Alaska before he and his girlfriend were eaten by one. Her reading raises not only various questions about the ethics of the director, that is, about the representation of the devoted idealist Treadwell, but also a question about the human and its relation to the animal-other. In challenging the centuries old habitual thinking of life in terms of binary oppositions resulting in the creation of boundaries, the essay discloses the anthropocentric attitude inherent in the hegemonizing discourses governing human and non-human animals.

Canan Şavkay's **The Precarious Position of Cats in Doris Lessing's *On Cats*** is a discussion of the literary possibilities of relating to non-human animals in alternative ways which are nonhegemonic and respectful of their alterity. Şavkay reads Lessing's text as a very emotional book evoking love and appreciation in the reader, while also drawing attention to the vulnerable position of cats who have become emotionally dependent on humans. Doris Lessing's *On Cats* is an account of a range of cats she has encountered over the years and taken care of. Şavkay's essay points at the ways in which Lessing employs a narrative strategy through which we are enabled to see the cat in a different light from our habitual ways of projecting human qualities onto animals. While adopting a relational role as narrator, Lessing opposes the humanist prioritization of autonomy and instead directs her reader's attention towards responsibility and appreciation for the animal's alterity. Although Lessing emphasizes the tangible aspect of cats' lives, she does not put them into the position of humanity's inferior other, but establishes an emotional bond between cat and human.

As such, Şavkay argues, Lessing subverts the humanist concept of Man as a rational and autonomous being and replaces it with a focus on our relational capacities. Lessing's representation of cats is therefore an indirect interrogation of humanist concepts.

Ferdi Çetin relocates the search for new representational strategies to rethink interconnectedness within a posthumanist framework from the literary to the theatrical. **Decentering the Human on Stage:** *Neither* **as Posthumanist Opera** reconsiders the history of the modernist stage with particular emphasis on the works of writers including Stein and Beckett as well as the contemporary theatrical practices of Goebbels and Castellucci, identifying as their common aspect a persistent effort to challenge the humanistic conception of "character". Çetin views Romeo Castellucci's production of Beckett's operatic text *Neither* as an experimental platform inviting the spectator subjects to negotiate new formations of subjectivity with what they see on stage; cats, sheep, mannequins, machines and robots. His reading of *Neither* as posthumanist opera celebrates the potential of the performing arts to decenter the human and produce new ways of being in an enlarged community "based on environmental interconnections".

The last piece in the book is about poetry, and what poetry has to offer in the way of creating that enlarged community. Özlem Karadağ's essay, **Ecofeminist Ecopoetics and Carol Ann Duffy** introduces a relatively new term, ecopoetics with a view to uniting it with ecofeminism, the feminist-environmental movement. Ecofeminist ecopoetics is thus both a way of writing poems and a critical approach to nature in poetry and literature. Karadağ's theoretical discussion shows the ways in which ecofeminist ecopoetics strives to trace and discuss ecofeminist patterns in text-making with specific focus on the use of language, subjects such as nature, nonhuman animals, and human others. The essay proposes that Duffyesque poetry, through a close reading of her selected poems with ecofeminism and ecopoetic, can be recognized as ecofeminist ecopoetics.

All the essays in this volume point out "interconnectedness" as a key concept in redefining the nature of our relations on this planet with nature and the environment, with other human and non-human animals and other forms of life. This immense web of interconnectedness at work including all the inhabitants of the earth and their naturecultural environment translates easily into what those of us in literary and cultural studies recognize as "intertextuality".[3] Not unlike the vast Borgesian library imagined to be containing all the books that have been written from the beginning of time, this web of innumerable textual links enables us to move freely from text to text and see interconnections where previously we had not. "The metaphor of the Text," Roland Barthes has famously written, "is that of the network; if the Text expands, it is by the effect of a combinative operation, of a systematics (an image, moreover, close to the views of contemporary biology concerning the living being)."[4] For any text can thus be considered the "co-text" of other texts, all of which then enter into an endless dialogic relationship within a context freed of hierarchical relationships. I hope that this selection of essays informed by contemporary theories which combine formalistic aesthetic analysis with political and ethical questions relevant to our present-day concerns will prove capable of engaging in further dialogs in far more creative ways.

---

3   The term was first coined by Julia Kristeva whose views drew on, and developed, Mikhail Bakhtin's theory of dialogism. For both Kristeva and Barthes, intertextuality means more than a mere postmodernist play of uncovering the references and allusions to other writings in a text. Hypothetically any discursive practice contains a plurality owing to textual interconnections which are inexhaustible because each reader comes to the text with their own set potential of interconnections.

4   Roland Barthes, "From Work to Text", *The Rustling of Language*, Richard Howard (*trs.*), Hill and Wang, 1986, 61.

Sinem Yazıcıoğlu

The Urban Body in Edgar Allan Poe's "The Man of the Crowd"

Jonathan Arac writes, "Poe's life is a tale of five cities: Boston, Richmond, Baltimore, Philadelphia, and New York" (63). Poe actually lived in these cities, and he also mentioned them in his writing; however, his relation to the city exceeds these five specific locations, and extends to the cities of the world, such as Bombay in "A Tale of the Ragged Mountains", Paris in "The Murder in the Rue Morgue" and "The Mystery of Marie Roget", and London in "The Man of the Crowd". Poe's cities are, therefore, generic settings that characterize the disquieting sensation of being witness to the process of social and industrial transformation in the nineteenth century. On the other hand, writing during the 1840s complicates Poe's depiction of the city, since at that time only a few American cities could match the density of population in Paris and London, and New York's grid system, for example, with its clarity and simplicity, presented a setback for the mysteries and terrors Poe has famously associated with the city. For this reason, Poe has chosen Paris and London for detailing the anxieties specific to the experiences within the urban environment.

"The Man of the Crowd" is one of Poe's urban stories, and addresses the characteristics of the metropolis more than any other of his works. Set in London, the story features a character observing the urban population, yet is drawn to the mysterious face of a man within the crowd and starts to follow his footsteps until he comes to the point of exhaustion and decides to abandon his efforts. The city of London might be an appropriate location for Poe's depiction of stratified urban society in the metropolis, yet the story also responds to the gradual transformation of American political discourse on the emergence of industrialization and urbanization throughout the nineteenth century. Early nineteenth-century ideals of the pastoral, epitomized by Thomas Jefferson's politics, had envisioned the United States as a purely agricultural country. In a letter from 1791, when he was the Secretary of State, Jefferson praises American economy, claiming that it depends on the American people's "conviction that a solid Union is the best rock of their safety, from the favorable seasons which for some years past have co-operated with a fertile soil and a genial climate to increase the production of agriculture", adding that "there is not a nation under the sun enjoying more present prosperity" (260). The images of nature even in the description of the state show that for Jefferson, American wealth and prosperity depended on its strict adherence to staying as a farming community and discouraging manufacture within the national borders. This political discourse aimed to maintain the imagined virtues of organic society, whose loss they witnessed in Europe with despise; however, as Richard Hofstadter posits, "The United States was born in the country and has moved to the city" (23). By the time Andrew Jackson took office in 1829, American political imagination could no longer contain the transformative forces resulting from technological inventions and the centralization of capital. The metropolis thus started to emerge by the mid-nineteenth century both with its prospects and complications.

Arguably the strongest and widest effect of the growing urbanization was the irreversible symbiosis between the human body and the metropolis. In *Flesh and Stone*, Richard Sennett argues that "a master image of the body" (23) was the foundational model for city planning. With a particular example on the scientific developments in medically understanding the human circulatory system, Sennett offers an analysis on the ways in which blood circulation and the interconnection of human veins had become a metaphor for Adam Smith's formulation for the flow of capital in *The Wealth of Nations*, while capitalism consequently required an urban space enabling an increased mobility of human bodies. However, as the human body became the initial form of the modern city, it was also compelled into constantly adapting to the increasing stimuli and flows within the urban environment, creating a persistent reciprocity. My focus in this essay will be on the relation between the human body and the metropolis as it presents itself in Edgar Allan Poe's "The Man of the Crowd". More specifically, I will address the narrator's observation of the city through human faces and his concentration on a man in the crowd, whom I consider the representation of the city. The historicity of British and American political discourses on the pastoral and the city will inform my analysis. As a result, I will argue that, by his use of a descent-and-return narrative and the doppelgänger in the context of urban environment, Poe reconfigures the crisis of urbanization into a bodily experience.

Not of London, But of the Soul

Upon his visit to Philadelphia, Charles Dickens wrote in his *American Notes*, "It is a handsome city, but distractingly regular. After walking about it for an hour or two, I felt that I would have given the world for a crooked street" (235). It is no surprise that the streets of Philadelphia, where Poe resided at the time when Dickens visited there, seemed neatly ordered to an author who had virtually mapped the urban landscape of the nineteenth-century London in his novels. Contrary to Dickens's description of Philadelphia, the London of his time was a complex network of urban population due to the rapid development of industrialization and the consequent mobility of rural populations to the metropolis. In *The Condition of Working Class in England* (1844), for example, Friedrich Engels expressed his amazement about the limitlessness of urban space:

> A town, such as London, where a man may wander for hours together without reaching the beginning of the end, without meeting the slightest hint which could lead to the inference that there is open country within reach, is a strange thing. This colossal centralization, this heaping together of two and a half millions of human beings at one point, has multiplied the power of this two and a half millions a hundredfold (328).

Engels's wandering man of London also observes "human turmoil" and "endless lines of vehicles" (329) as well as poverty, which "often dwells in hidden alleys close to the palaces of the rich; but, in general, a separate territory has been assigned to it, where [...] it may struggle along as it can" (331). This partitioning of the city and its slums is constantly complicated by the slums' "immense tangle of streets" and "hundreds and thousands of alleys and courts" (333). The center, in other words, develops inconsistent tangles and sequestered spots within, resembling the veins of the human body and the blood pumping through them, making it harder to comprehend the totality of the city. In a city thus organized, the employed part of the dense and mobile urban population became pedestrians or commuters, while the rest were considered vagrants. In *London Labour and the London Poor*, for example, Henry Mayhew described London's vagrant population satirically as "the wandering tribes of this country" and "the nomadic races of England" (2). From a different perspective, Engels complains about the "brutal indifference, the unfeeling isolation" of Londoners and asserts that "the dissolution of mankind into monads, of which each one has a separate principle, the world of atoms, is here carried out to its utmost extreme" (329).

The chronicles of urban life in London during the 1840s show that this wandering man is compelled to be disoriented, since the organization of the metropolis has caused one to be atomized and one's senses to disperse all over urban life and urban population, hampering any concentrated effort to make sense of the stimuli and comprehend its connections to the body of the city. Nineteenth-century literature on both sides of the Atlantic has thus proliferated with narratives directly addressing this phenomenon, expressing the middle-class anxiety and working-class exhaustion of living in the metropolis. The emergence of crime fiction and the development of the detective and criminal figures, the themes of alienation and isolation, the depiction of cramped, smoky and dark interiors all resonate with the urban transformation of the period. Furthermore, while the incomprehensibility of urban life called for a rational organizing mind as that of crime fiction's detective, the ills of the metropolis equally aroused desire for those who either lived in the city but avoided contact with its dark side, or resided in the rural provinces and was curious about the city. The city guidebook consequently emerged as a new genre; yet among them, George Foster's books deviate from the conventional detached and informative narratives and provide a ground view of New York even to its underbelly. However apologetic Foster sounds as he explains in the preface of *Celio, or New York Above Ground and Underground* that he has a specific moral in his writing, and he believes that "vice and misery are not necessary result [sic] of human life in this world; and that were human nature not distorted, evil would not exist" (4), he has evoked erotic associations for the city's underground, satisfied the desire and curiosity for learning about all aspects of the city, and created a demand for the circulation of urban evils.

Edgar Allan Poe's "The Man of the Crowd" is contemporary with the above-mentioned concerns and accounts of urban life, and directly addresses the city's incomprehensibility. For the Baltimore-born Virginian residing in Philadelphia, the city could not be summed up to a local place; he rather held it as a categorical and transnational space. For this reason, his depiction of London in the story is not strictly place-bound, but resonates with the transformation of urban environment and anxieties arising from it. Poe's treatment of space has been likewise subject to Jonathan Arac's categorization of American literary canon in terms of local, personal and literary narratives. For Arac, Poe's works fit into personal narratives, which "characteristically have the circular shape of descent and return to the elevation of ordinary civilized life" (77); instead of using particular places to represent the local color, Poe's fiction prioritizes the personal journey of arriving, traversing and returning from real or imagined spaces. The city in this sense is an apt location for Poe's poetics of quest, as in the descending movement from the streets of an Italian city to the wine cellar in "The Cask of Amontillado", adapting a personal descent-and-return to murder with impunity.

The story starts with a two-step introduction: Firstly, the narrator addresses the impossibility of solving mysteries by the trope of reading, referring to an anonymous German book; secrets are in this sense are likened to books which resist the reader. However, the epigraph from La Bruyère's *The Characters, or the Manners of the Age* at the beginning, which can be translated as "It is a great misfortune not to be alone", relates the trope of reading to the interpretation of man's physical appearance and behavior, which is gradually adapted to the interpretation of the city. The French and German references in the story's opening establish the modern urban anxiety towards the individual's criminal potentials due to the disorganized, tangled and hidden spaces of the metropolis. The second part of the introduction moves from abstract ideas to the narrator himself, in an almost descending form. From the narrator's account, a previous descent and return pattern is revealed: Having recovered from his ill health, the narrator has returned to the prospects of life and positions himself in a busy coffee-house in London, reading the newspaper, observing the people inside and starting to look outside.

What is significant in the coffee-house, however, is the description of his "calm and inquisitive interest" (475) within a closed space: In the narrator's words, he is sitting "at the large bow-window" of the coffee-house; after his recovery, he finds enjoyment even in breathing indoors, and looks through "the smoky panes" (475). Although the people inside are described as "promiscuous", they are also "company", indicating the narrator's understanding of urban socialization in the form of collective and detached relations, and implying a controlled upper-middle-class desire for promiscuity since his inquisitive interest extends well beyond the window pane. The inside therefore provides a secure yet limited urban environment, illustrated with his position behind the smoky bow-window in the shape of an eye-ball; in other words, the allusion to the cataract eye reveals the means of mediation by which the narrator will observe and comprehend the city from a closed space.

As the narrator's gaze shifts to the outside, he observes a much more diverse crowd that makes up the urban population. In the narrator's words, the crowd is comprised of "two dense and continuous tides of population" and "the tumultuous sea of human heads" (475) who are "the throng" (475) in "aggregate relations" (476). Aside from the variety of words used for the urban masses, the narrator notices their intensification as it becomes darker, implying their crowding during rush hours. The narrator's linguistic investment on describing them shows that the people outside represent a wider diversity incomparable to the "promiscuous company" within, yet they also gradually evoke his anxiety as his description centers on the crowd's irregular movements. It is at this point that the narrator is carried along with the circulation of the urban population and starts to "[descend] into details" (476) to observe the singular faces within the crowd, which starts the descent-and-return narrative.

The position of the narrator's first gaze illustrates Michel de Certeau's reading of the urban environment, which theorizes the signification of spatial practices within the city, particularly the act of walking. De Certeau's argument on walking in the city actually starts with the description of a distanced and elevated position which he associates with the gaze of the voyeur, similar to Poe's narrator in the story. From this perspective, the voyeur is removed from the masses and the present stimuli, which makes it possible to observe the city in its totality in a way to provide the optical opportunity to map the city. However, de Certeau finds that the voyeur position is an abstraction, intending to give the city a geometrical order; reduced from the body to the observing eye, the voyeur represses the temporality, vitality and energy of the city. Consequently, for de Certeau, the city observed from such position is "a picture, whose condition of possibility is an oblivion and a misunderstanding of practices" (93). What seems like the map of the city is nothing but a misrepresentation of its dynamics. As the narrator becomes interested in observing the individual bodies in the crowd rather than the collective and uncountable company inside, his observation and interpretation are simultaneously urbanized, because, typical of urban experience, his attention is no longer concentrated, but dispersed to the pedestrians outside.

Classifying the Urban Population

For his observation of the faces, the narrator uses the pseudo-scientific discourse of the nineteenth century in his process of rationalizing the urban environment, particularly physiognomy and phrenology. In *Phrenology in Connection with the Study of Physiognomy* (1826), Johann Gaspar Spurzheim justified the validity of his theories in connection to the idea that "man is a unit" (383) and "each isolated part indicates the configuration as a whole" (382). In other words, by conducting a comparative study on the parts and proportions of the human body, Spurzheim claimed that it was possible to extract information regarding one's mind and character. Spurzheim's theory was popularized both in Britain and the United States within a cultural climate that praised the individual in the context of the Romantic celebration of organic unity and the American national narrative on individualism, observed by Alexis de Tocqueville in *Democracy in America*. The theory, however, also shows a growing need for rationalizing and categorizing the human body against the failure of previous rational and scientific models, especially due to the fact that individuals in the urban environment are compelled into being social beings. Furthermore, although the individuals in the metropolis are atomized beings, their physical appearances have been complicated by the material conditions of their employment. Engels, for example, detailed the physical deterioration of the working class with a special emphasis on the deformation of the human skeletal system. Similarly, Karl Marx's famous metaphor of the capitalist as the vampire who "lives only by sucking living labour, and lives the more, the more labour it sucks" (342) illustrates the idea that the traces of capitalism are inscribed on the worker's body.

More than a phrenologist's pseudo-scientific reasoning, the narrator's gaze represents the amazement and disconcertment surfacing at the moment of observing the city as a social environment. This phenomenon resonates with the modern impulse to gather the senses as they disperse over the urban body. Walter Benjamin, who theorized the industrialized and urbanized gaze of modernity, has shown the ways in which, as a result, the relation between the art work and its audience has been irreparably broken by what he calls the loss of aura. My aim in citing Benjamin in this context is not to say that the urban masses can be considered a modern art work, but rather because the narrator's gaze functions in the same way as the soon-to-emerge filmic art since his descriptions are sequentially edited as of montage while he is watching them from behind the window frame. Within this sequence, however, faces are brought closer to depict instances which represent the diversity of the crowd, echoing in Benjamin's words "the desire of contemporary masses to bring things 'closer' spatially and humanly" (217). Although the narrator views the masses through the norms of his own judgment in his comfort zone, his view is compelled into an urban form, moving him to a liminal position between the inside and the outside, and implying the potential of his being part of the crowd.

The narrator's description starts with the "decent" group comprised of "noblemen, merchants, attorneys, tradesmen, stock-jobblers" (476) who are portrayed as mechanical figures characterized by their automatic and indifferent movements. This is the only group the narrator openly says "[t]hey did not greatly excite my attention" (476), and he quickly shifts the eyes towards the group of clerks, who are described less by their movements than their physical appearances. With their "bright boots, well-oiled hair, and supercilious lips" and "affectation of respectability" (476), the clerks represent the mechanical reproduction of genteel manners and tastes, which implies the narrator's disapproval for their pretense. The narrator does not interpret the manners of the businessmen and the clerks further, since their looks have already been inscribed with class distinction and their superficiality demands immediate displacement; consequently, he continues displacing his attention to other classes of individuals.

Following the two "decent" groups, the narrator's tone and discourse changes as he starts observing the lower classes. Although he finds the appearance of pickpockets "dashing" (476), he describes them as a "race

[...] with which all great cities are infested" (476). Another group similarly treated as the pickpockets is the gamblers, whose faces betray "a certain sodden swarthiness of complexion, a filmy dimness of eye, and pallor and compression of lip" (477). The narrator's description is significant in that after his observation of two groups of urban professionals and before moving to urban labor, he regards pickpocketing and gambling as urban occupations, which have a similar organization to that of a profession. Both pickpocketing and gambling are also described in terms of their invasiveness by the troublesome swarming of the pickpockets and the influence of gambling on the dandies and the military men, who fall to the habit as "prey" (477). The unsung parasite metaphor problematizes the lack of balance between ill-deserved gain and unplanned loss by risk-taking, and when read as an inverted version of Marx's vampire metaphor, reveals the narrator's concern about the physical and economic vulnerability of upper-middle-class urban population.

The narrator's description of the urban poor is ambiguous, since he considers lower class urban professionals, the unemployed, the invalid, the vagrant, the skilled and unskilled manual workers, employed or unemployed women in the same category, which offers him "darker and deeper themes of speculation" (477). Portraying the wretched faces of the city, the narrator therefore focuses not specifically on class but on capitalism's physical effects on the urban poor. Described as the most mobile portion of the urban masses, their ambiguity, poverty and diversity also intensify the narrative pace, since the narrator starts shifting his attention even more rapidly, observing a larger number of faces among them. Contrary to the other groups of people who can be interpreted by the details in their costumes and gestures, the urban poor signify the void through which the narrator can experience the depths of the descent he desires.

Compelled into constantly displacing his attention to another, the narrator finally notices the man of the crowd, who "arrested and absorbed" (478) his attention. In other words, the narrator considers the man of the crowd an irresistible void to discover. Finding on his face not one but several simultaneous expressions, he develops "a craving desire to keep the man in view" (478) and leaves the coffee-house for the street. The narrator's desire to see the man in close resonates with Benjamin's assertion that the masses want to overcome the distance from objects. De Certeau also maintains that a ground view is necessary to make sense of the city, because it is a place produced by a myriad of pedestrians whose acts are considered speech acts. De Certeau writes that the pedestrians' "swarming mass is an innumerable collection of singularities. Their intertwined paths give their shape to spaces. They weave places together" (97); similar to the construction of language, the urban environment is based on a constant choice of selection and combination by bodily movements, making it a spatial signifying machine. In order to decipher this language, the narrator goes out for closer observation.

While the narrator's quest starts with observing "the absolute idiosyncrasy" (478) of expression in the man's face, his walking in the city gradually dissolves their difference. Firstly, by approaching him, he integrates himself to the crowd and becomes part of the masses. Although his description of the man starts with his physical weakness and dirty garments, as the opposite of the narrator's social status, it is this nameless individual character whom the narrator desires to know about. As the truly urban character, the man of the crowd illustrates the abolishing of the difference between the controlled interior and the chaotic exterior in the urban environment, and is thus portrayed as a character whose body transcends temporal and spatial limits. With his roquelaure, an unusual garment for nineteenth century London, and the diamond and dagger the narrator claims to notice inside his cloak, the man encapsulates the complexities and anxieties urban environment evokes. Secondly, to stay unnoticed, the narrator starts to follow his footsteps and guides himself to the parts of the city beyond the thoroughfare. Repeating the man's movements around the city, and realizing that the man is retracing his own steps, the narrator witnesses the city's being written and rewritten like a palimpsest, yet fails to notice he is forced to adopt the language himself.

Peeping through the City's Cracks

Robert Tally has elaborated on the structure of descent-and-return narrative in Edgar Allan Poe's stories by giving special emphasis on their discovery process and narrative pace, naming it "Poe's poetics of descent" (85). The descent in "The Man of the Crowd" likewise causes a gradually increasing pace, starting with the narrator's ideas and his stagnant position and gradually shifting to the energy of the streets. As the man walks, he makes denser urban locations more visible, such as the avenue, street shops, and theaters, as well as deserted lanes, as if to compose a population density map by his footsteps. However, the narrative pace of the story momentarily halts when the narrator follows the man to the peripheries of the city and notices that "the paving-stones lay at random, displaced from their beds by the rankly-growing grass" (481). Although the grass is a common plant, the narrator's realization of it shows they have reached the possible end of the city, and that traces of nature are resurfacing. The scandalous moment of seeing grass underneath the pavement also alludes to the erotic repulsion and attraction at seeing the human pubic hair, and genders the body of the city for the first time, since it locates the direction of the city's growth from the rural exterior to the urban center, the assault on natural environment by industrialization and urbanization, and the averted desire for sensual urban pleasures. Poe's adoption of a poetic discourse in his description of the grass also means to add tension to the moment of this observation, increasing the narrator's anxiety and repulsion. In this specific neighborhood, he also observes "large bands of the most abandoned of a London populace" around "tall, antique, worm-eaten, wooden tenements" (481) in a moment of encounter with the urban poor he has not seen in the city center. The location of the grass, therefore, marks the urban gateway for mobility, expansion and perversion, and signifies the social and economic costs of urbanization.

Although located in the slums of London, the grass in "The Man of the Crowd" echoes the nineteenth-century American political imagination of the pastoral as well. Until its wide range of political associations of democracy, plurality and unity in Walt Whitman's *Leaves of Grass*, which postdates Poe's story, the grass appears as the liminal space bordering the pleasurable landscape, the garden, or the perilous wilderness. The literary repercussions of this discourse can be seen in Poe's own "Descent into the Maelstrom", whose first-person narrator advises the traveller "Now raise yourself up a little higher – hold on to the grass, if you feel giddy – so – and look out, beyond the belt of vapor beneath us, into the sea" (128). Up to that point, the traveller struggles to walk over the cliff, which arises on "the world of crags beneath" him, yet his fear is that "the very foundations of the mountain were in danger from the fury of the winds"

(127). In a setting where the ground is equally hostile and insecure as the air, that ascent is as threatening as descent, the traveller is commanded by the voice of experience and authority to remain closer to the grass, yet discouraged to be likewise rooted. At the outer thresholds of civilization and wilderness, the grass therefore provides a solid, yet temporary protection, since the traveller needs to elevate himself to observe the sea from the top of the mountain and fulfill the purpose of his visit.

Poe has also used the grass imagery to encapsulate the buffer zone between European settlements and indigenous populations in the context of Westward Expansion. Particularly in "A Tale of the Ragged Mountains", the character Bedloe takes his routine morning walk "among the chain of wild and dreary hills that lie westward and southward of Charlottesville" (680) where his own descent-and-return narrative starts with remembering the "strange stories" of "the uncouth and fierce races of men who tenanted their groves and caverns" (681) and hearing first the drums and then "a wild rattling or jingling sound" (682). Securing himself beneath the tree, he sees a shadow on the grass, which leads him into his mesmeric experience. Furthermore, in "The System of Doctor Tarr and Professor Fether", the narrator and his travelling companion start their brief journey to the private asylum by leaving the main road for "a grass-grown path, which, in half an hour, nearly lost itself in a dense forest, clothing the base of a mountain" (307). The treatment of the grass in these examples show that the grass is an essentially spatial configuration, separating civilization from the wilderness, while revealing the vulnerability of utopian fantasies and the pitfalls of American development. The grass therefore epitomizes the ambiguity arising from the momentary realization of being at the edge of the void and having to leave it only to return with the experience gained.

Similar to Poe's other stories mentioned above, reaching the grass marks the point of the narrator's return in "The Man of the Crowd". From this point onwards, the man starts walking even more haphazardly, "backward and forward, without apparent object" (481). His "half shriek of joy" and "mad energy" (481) correspond to the instant shocks upon perceiving unexpected urban stimuli. However, from the narrator's perspective, it is not the man who is responding to these shocks; by changing the scale of his previous verbal expression of interest from his being "arrested and absorbed" to his interest's "all-absorbing" (481) quality, the narrator grants himself the position of a sensual subject and consequently deems the man senseless. Considering the man's constant movement without exhaustion and all the senses activated in the narrator, it is true that the man cannot be defined by his sensuality. From the beginning of his quest, the narrator's leaving his position behind the window frame and following the man might have opened his senses to all the stimuli in the city; conversely, the man of the crowd evokes sensations, but does not feel. As Sennett argues, "Moving around freely diminishes sensory awareness, arousal by places or the people in those places. Any strong visceral connection to the environment threatens to tie the individual down [...] to move around freely, you can't feel too much" (256). What makes the man of the crowd competent in his mobility is that he is in fact the flesh and blood of the city and that his constant and senseless movements embody the urban environment.

Poe's treatment of the man's body as the city renders the narrator's relation to the city ambiguous. On the one hand, he responds critically and thus detaches himself from what he observes; on the other hand, he traces and retraces the man's footsteps. His pursuit even goes to the extremes of imitating him: The moment he sees the man in roquelaure, he wears his overcoat; as the man constantly avoids full visibility with his irregular movements, he covers his face with a handkerchief; he increases his pace to be able to follow him. Furthermore, he has a casual and infrequent use of the first-person plural pronoun, which is repeated twice as the only subject of a sentence towards the end. Informed by the similarities between the narrator and the man, it is possible to read the narrator's momentary vision of the dagger and diamond not only as evidence of crime, but as reflecting objects. The recurring trope of the double (doppelgänger) in Poe's fiction emerges here as an experience inherent to the city, where the subject externalizes the troubles of urban life and projects an urban self, responds to it as an external object with amazement and anxiety, studies it closely only to discover that his self and its urban other are identical. The descent-and-return pattern becomes the narrator's process of acknowledging the complications of the city, embodied by the man of the crowd who represents his urban self.

Unable to complete his return from descent with an enlightened consciousness, or in this case, to re-internalize his troublesome urban self, the narrator announces the end of his pursuit. At this point, he associates him with a "deep crime" (481) he could not solve, for he failed to comprehend the man's motives. The story finally restores the initial trope of reading by suggesting that it is impossible to 'read' the man. As a result, the return of the descent narrative is realized not by the narrator's newly gained ability to unite his two selves, but by his acknowledgment that his urban self will essentially remain incomprehensible to him. Like the circulation of blood in the human body, the non-thinking, non-feeling yet constantly acting urban self functions independently from the reflecting and perceiving subject, and coerces him into imitated action. In "The Man of the Crowd", therefore, Poe molds the problems of urban life, such as the crisis of urbanization, the incomprehensibility of the city, and the anxieties resulting from all such effects into the form of the human body.

Works Cited

Arac, Jonathan. *The Emergence of American Literary Narrative, 1820–1860*. Harvard UP, 2005.

Benjamin, Walter. *Illuminations*. Pimlico, 1999.

De Certeau, Michel. *The Practice of Everyday Life*. University of California Press, 1988.

Dickens, Charles. *American Notes for General Circulation Volume 1*. Cambridge UP, 2009.

Engels, Friedrich. *The Condition of the Working Class in England in 1844*. George Allen and Unwin, 1952.

Foster, George. *Celio: or New York Above Ground and Underground*. Dewitt & Davenport, 1850.

Hofstadter, Richard. *The Age of Reform*. Knopf, 1963.

Jefferson, Thomas. *The Writings of Thomas Jefferson Volume 3*. Cambridge UP, 2011.

Marx, Karl. *Capital Volume I*. Penguin, 1990.

Mayhew, Henry. *London Labour and the London Poor*. Griffin, Bohn and Company, 1861.

Poe, Edgar Allan. *The Complete Tales and Poems of Edgar Allan Poe*. The Modern Library, 1965.

Sennett, Richard. *Flesh and Stone*. Norton, 1996.

Spurzheim, J. G. "from *Phrenology in Connection with the Study of Physiognomy.*" *Literature and Science in the Nineteenth Century: An Anthology*, edited by Laura Otis, Oxford UP, 2002, pp. 382–6.

Tally, Robert. "Irreversible Narrative in Poe's "M.S. Found in a Bottle." *Studies in Irreversibility: Texts and Contexts*, edited by Benjamin Schreier, Cambridge Scholars, 2007, pp. 83–98.

İnci Bilgin Tekin

An Old Debate, New Perspectives: Cherrie Moraga's and Caryl Churchill's Dialogues with Nature

"On or about December 1910 human nature changed" as the celebrated feminist writer Virginia Woolf notes in her comprehensive essay
"Mr Bennett and Mrs Brown", published in 1924. Woolf's observation
is directly linked to the rise of modernism which is both the consequence
and reinforcer of technology and urbanization. From classical antiquity
to romanticism, from neo-classicism to modernism, literary history has
reflected man's attempts to understand "nature" in a strong dialogue with
its supposed opposite "culture", which is innately man-made. To recall the
great Romantic poet William Wordsworth who vividly describes the post-
industrialization experience:

> The world is too much with us; late and soon,
> Getting and spending, we lay waste our powers;-
> Little we see in Nature that is ours;
> We have given our hearts away, a sordid boon! (L 1–4)

As Wordsworth's lines imply, alienation from nature ends up in self-al-
ienation. Obsessed with finding means to control its supposedly antagonist, nature, man has reinforced industrialization over and over without
noticing his loss of connection with his own earthly roots.

Rising in the 21st century, ecocriticism basically criticizes this wholly
"anthropocentric" process which Timothy Clark relates to viewing the
world as a potential "resource" for human beings. (2) In other words,
ecocriticism makes a call for rethinking the environment outside human-
centered contexts.

The classical association of "nature" with women and "culture" with
men, can be traced to Greek mythology in which mother goddess Gaia
symbolizes the earth and fertility. Her son Zeus's, the chief god of the
twelve Olympians', taking over is usually identified with the initiation of
a patriarchal system as it coincides with early Greek city states structure.

> First follow NATURE, and your judgment frame
> By her just standard, which is still the same (L 1,2)

In these frequently quoted lines, the great Augustan Age poet and critic Alexander Pope also uses "her", the feminine possessive pronoun, to refer to nature. Given this context, "culture" which usually signifies a male-centered power division, has continuously reinforced patriarchy and vice versa. Coined by the French critic Françoise d'Eaubonne, the term "eco-feminism" incorporates "ecology" and "feminism". Rising in late 1970s, this movement specifically studies the relationship between women and nature from the perspective of equality and underlines the necessity for collaboration (Merchant 193–218).

Cherrie Moraga and Caryl Churchill are two inspiring contemporary women dramatists coming from American and English backgrounds. The Chicana lesbian feminist playwright, theorist and drama teacher Cherrie Moraga is known for her political activism as well. The well-known English feminist playwright Caryl Churchill is also noted as a political activist. Moraga and Churchill have a common growing interest in representing issues about the environment. They both plot "Heroes and Saints" (1992) and "The Skriker" (1994) around mankind's earthly and celestial connection to nature. Moraga and Churchill's plays also own strong feminist discourses.

In *Heroes and The Saints* and *The Skriker*, Moraga and Churchill manifest their ecofeminist perspectives in incorporating American and British mythologies into their environmentalist contexts. The setting in *Heroes and Saints* is a valley around central California, where Mexican origined Americans (Chicanos) work in planting. However where they work is thoroughly polluted by toxic pesticides and chemicals. As a consequence of over-pollution, cancer and other diseases are very common among town's children and adults. Born as a head without body, the central character of the play, Cerezita, is one of the victims of this situation. The town starts to protest the severe conditions by using media to show the victims so that they would catch public attention. However the play ends without any resolution as the situations get even worse to lead to the death of all townspeople.

Taking place in the local setting of a fictional town in California, *Heroes and Saints* represents a time when nature was thoroughly lost and outside smelled dirt rather than fresh air. Born as a head due to excessive use of pesticides, Moraga's heroine, Cerezita, also serves as a metaphor for all the innocent victims of the new world: Babies born disabled, children dying of cancer, the ethnically oppressed Chicana, as well as the poor. Cerezita in *Heroes and Saints* echo Moraga's perspective in saying "our law states that no rich can enter heaven without the poor taking him by the hand" (101) Cerezita is often attributed a mythical association, likened by Moraga to "pre-Columbian Olmecas". Reminiscent of Biblical myths, she also appears in the image of Virgin de Guadalupe (Virgin Mary in Mexican context). That the priest takes advise from Cerezita supports this biblical allusion. In this respect, Cerezita signifies hope, a possible "second coming" (91) of nature.

Reminding of English folk legends, Churchill's Skriker is an ever-transforming ancient Fairy, coming from the underworld, to enslave two young pregnant women, Josie and Lily, in a lust for love and revenge. As Josie attempts to burn her baby in the oven, she is sent to a mental hospital. There Josie is visited by Lily. Skriker disguises herself firstly as one of the patients in the hospital, a middle-aged woman. Josie's sister Lily, also pregnant, asks Skriker's help for Josie's mental recovery. However, Skriker wishes to get Lily's child. The Skriker searches for attachment in approaching Josie and Lily. However, this wish is never fulfilled even if Skriker continuously changes form among male and female, young and old, human and nonhuman entities. Skriker makes Josie and Lily accompany her to the underworld where tested by Skriker in personal integrity, neither of the girls is strong enough to survive. Skriker is a play without any scene or act changes which implies that similar to the main character, Skriker, the play is not bound to the idea of character or setting change. Moraga's journey starts with the local context of California region while Churchill addresses a more universal concern by denying to fix in one setting and time. However both plays commonly underline different but parallel consequences of mankind's destruction of nature while the writerly motivation of these two playwrights highlight women's potential to unite with nature by making an ecofeminist call. Drawing on the early female image of a fertile mother goddess Gaia, symbolized by the earth, one could trace Moraga and Churchill's writerly motivations to women's potential to reproduce and produce rather than consume and destroy.

Moraga and Churchill's plays reflect the whole age's search for root-edness and relatedness by uniting with nature and therefore revisiting classical mythology the legends and stories of which, as Edith Hamilton suggests, depict the young times of the world when man lived at the heart of nature. (13) Association of each one of the twelve Olympian deities with certain aspects of nature supports this idea. For instance in Homer's *Odyssey*, the rewarding Athena reflects the protective side of nature while the punishing Poseidon stands for the destructive aspect of nature.

Cherrie Moraga's play's emphasis on nature proceeds in dialogues with native American mythology. For instance, Cerezita asks Mario to tell the story about the Mayan god. (104) Similarly, notes on Cerezita include a comparison to pre-Columbian Olmecas. The quote Moraga places before the play, "Aztlan belongs to those who plant the seeds, water the fields and gather the crops" also introduces a mythical allusion while Aztlan signifies the legendary homeland of the Aztec. Aztlan which the Chicana feminist theorist Gloria Anzaldua relates to their "lost land", California (23–31), dwells at the heart of Moraga's play. Revisiting Aztlan with environmental consciousness, Moraga reads the mythical land as a place where the Chicano people are exposed to white American, or as the Chicanos call them "Gringo", oppression. Moraga also views the excessive use of pesticides in San Joaquin Valley, which is close to the Mexican-American border, where the majority of inhabitants are the "red" (Moraga 148), as a sign of this oppression.

Caryl Churchill's title strongly implies a reference to British folkloric figure, skriker. Patricia Monaghan defines the legendary "skriker" as a "shape-shifting", "ever-transforming" fairy, usually associated with the strong scream heard in Lancashire and Yorkshire forests. (421) In some British folk legends, Skriker is also depicted as a banshee spirit, a sign of deadly menace. Caryl Churchill authentically dramatizes this mythical entity of the Irish and the Northern English as a supernatural character. The play also introduces other characters from British folklore such as Yallery Brown, Kelpie, Jennie Greenteeth, Rawhead and bloodybones, BlackAnnis, and the Spriggan. These characters are presented as other inhabitants of the underworld, where Skriker comes from.

As Amelie Howe Kritzer notes, Caryl Churchill's Skriker can be traced not only to Irish and Northern English but also to West African myths.

(112) While Kritzer relates Churchill's Skriker to a well-known spider-like, anthropomorphic trickster figure, Anansi, Skriker's ever signifying language and ever transforming appearance are also reminiscent of two other African trickster figures of signifying monkey and Esu-Elegbara, respectively. Henri Louis Gates relates the ever-signifying language of African American literary tradition to the trickster figure, signifying monkey, of the African vernacular and argues that African American literature, continuously signifies on the Euro-centric canon. Similarly, Gates considers Esu as a signifier of "double-voiced utterance". (52–59) Churchill's Skriker signifies duality in incorporating both sides of the binary opposites in its appearance such as male and female, young and old, human and nonhuman. In this respect, Skriker signifies on its own Other, human beings, by making their conceptions of identity destabilized. Skriker's habitat is destroyed and the damaged language speaks this broken experience in the form of run-on sentences and fragments:

> Don't get this ointment disappointment in your eyes I say to the mortal middle wife but of course she does and the splendoured thing palace picture palace winter policeman's ball suddenly blurred visionary missionary mishmash potato, and there was a mud hit mad hut and the mother a murder in rags tags and bob's your uncle and the baby a wrinkly crinkly crackerjack of all trading places, because of course it was all a glamour amour amorphous fuss about nothing. (8)

The run on statements which are hardly in the form of regular sentences can frequently beobserved in Skriker's speeches. "Mud" and "murder", "policeman" and "mishmash potato" coming together do not easily lead to a logical statement. However, Skriker's language in the form of non-ending statements signifies connectedness of nature.

On the other hand, fragments in Skriker's "damaged" language reflect the broken experience due to human intervention. The repetitive use of "but" above which leads to no logical connection as well as arbitrary word abbreviations like "b", display cutting off from the roots.

> But she never lets on so she gets home safe and sound the trumpet. But one day I'm in the market with b and put it in the oven helping myself and she sees me and says how's your wife waif and stray how's the baby? And I say what eye do you seize me with? This eye high diddley, she says. So I point my finger a thing at her and strike her blind alley cat o' nine tails (8)

On the other hand, Skriker's ever-transforming quality alludes to Esu which Gates attributes complex meditative roles for its contradictory characteristics (7). Skriker's body implies softness as it can easily transform while on the contrary her spirit is rigid. In this respect Skriker alludes to the Scottish legendary figure, Beira the Queen of Winter. In Scottish mythology, Beira stands for the chief goddess, mother and teacher to all other Scottish deities, the strongest of them all. While Beira's body is covered with soft snow and signifies the cycle of the seasons, Beira is often described as a scary figure for all other seasons. Involving the mission to teach, Beira's sense of motherhood can lead to both reward and punishment. One can also note a parallelism between Skriker's gradual and strategical enslavement of pregnant women and Beira's plans to dominate the other seasons. Although close to human conception of evil at first sight, Skriker indeed is motivated by a strong resentment toward the human race who destroyed Skriker's habitat: Given this context, Skriker's search for connection with Josie and Lily can be likened to the early generation mother's search for genuine communication with her children. Her motherly connection can be supported by her intention to take Lily's baby. Similar to Skriker, Beira has a deep search for love and affection while their motivation for revenge is dissatisfaction of these emotions. Standing for the dual opposites of nature, good and evil, winter and underworld embody both softness, productivity and harshness, darkness.

While Churchill's Skriker is a metaphor for the revenge of nature, Moraga's Cerezita serves as a metaphor for the birth of disabled children around San Joaquin Valley due to excessive use of pesticides. However, Cerezita is also attributed a fantastic quality as a head cannot survive without major parts of the body. In this respect, *Heroes and Saints* problematizes the conventional understanding of human shape in a body. In her following notes on Cerezita, Moraga asserts that her character should be thought as a posthuman rather than a human:

> CEREZITA is a head of human dimension, but one who possesses such dignity of bearing and classical Indian beauty she can, at times, assume nearly religious proportions. (The huge head figures of the pre-Columbian Olmecas are an apt comparison.) This image, however, should be contrasted with the very real "humanness" she exhibits on a daily functioning level.

> Her mobility and its limits are critical aspects of her character. For most of
> the play, CEREZITA is positioned on a rolling, table-like platform, which
> will be referred to as her "raite" (ride). It is automated by a button that
> operates with her chin. [...] (90)

That Moraga always writes Cerezita's name in capital letters also
contributes to this depiction. Shape shifting, Churchill's supernatural character Skriker can also be read as a metaphor for the posthuman. Churchill
defines Skriker whom she introduces in the underworld as "a shapeshifter
and death portent, ancient and damaged." (7) Skriker utters "Revengeance
is gold mine, sweet" (9) before meeting Josie and Lily in the form of an old
lady who needs their help. The genderless Skriker can easily transform into
a middle-aged man, a young lady, a child, even a non-living entity so as to
enslave the two young pregnant women gradually. In this respect, the play
problematizes the traditional understanding of one body as one form. The
choice of two teenage pregnant women, Josie and Lily, as Skriker's victims
also contribute to this perspective by signifying bodily growth, in turn
transformation. Josie and Lily's bodies continue to transform both due to
pregnancy and adolescence.

> One impulse from a vernal wood
> May teach you more of man,
> Of moral evil and of good,
> Than all the sages can (L 21–24)

The above lines by William Wordsworth highlight the didactic quality
of nature which the Olympian deities also represent. Lost on his way to
Ithaca from Troy, for instance, Odysseus was initially tested on his personal integrity and then taught moral lessons by Poseidon all through the
sea voyage. He was finally rewarded by Athena and sent back to Ithaca
safe. Cerezita is assigned by Moraga to teach a moral lesson to humanity
with her saint-like presentation in stage directions: "CEREZITA enters in
shadow. She is transfixed by the image of crucifixion". (92) Skriker tests
Lily and Josie's personal integrities all through the play and firstly punishes
Josie. While Lily is good to Skriker until the very end, Josie cannot hide her
hatred towards Skriker. In this respect, Skriker owns a didactic mission in
applying tests, rewards and punishments.

Nature was often personalized in canonical literature as a teacher
who effectively uses reward and punishment to reinforce man's behavior.

However, nature which entails duality by incorporating good and evil, light and dark, beautiful and ugly; in other words order and chaos, has been attributed both positive and negative qualities from the perspective of men. History has witnessed man's everlasting desire for power on a long list of entities involving nature. In this respect, certain aspects of nature including disasters and epidemic as well as unexpected encounters with the supernatural, which transcend the limits of cultural knowledge due to their chaotic or uncontrollable qualities, have gradually become the "Other", a tool for man's oppression. Skriker indeed represents the resentful side of the oppressed nature and, in turn, becomes an oppressor to take revenge. Death which Skriker signifies is the most negative concept man can ever imagine. However given the context of nature within the margins of which Skriker must be thought, death and birth, both related to bodily transformation, are not that distinct. Skriker dwells at the crossroads of the two by enslaving pregnant women. Similarly, CEREZITA represents the consequences of man's oppression of nature which Moraga describes as:

> The hundreds of miles of soil that surround the lives of Valley dwellers should not be confused with land. What was once land has become dirt, overworked dirt, overirrigated dirt, injected with deadly doses of chemicals and violated by every manner of the dirt do not call what was once the land their enemy. They remember what land used to be and await its second coming. (91)

The following lines of Skriker in the form of a man in 30s refers to a similar time when there is no longer a familiar world:

> Have you noticed the large number of meteorological phenomena lately? Earthquakes. Volcanoes. Drought. Apocalyptic meteorological phenomena. The increase of sickness. It was always possible to think whatever your personal problem, there's always nature. Spring will return even if it's without me. Nobody loves me but at least it's a sunny day. This has been a comfort to people as long as they've existed. But it's not available any more. Sorry. Nobody loves me and the sun's going to kill me. Spring will return and nothing will grow. Some people might feel concerned about that. But it makes me feel important. I'm going to be around when the world as we know it ends. I'm going to witness unprecedented catastrophe. [...] (38)

These lines depict the disturbing scenes surrounding the new reality of the world, the Anthropocene. Given this context, with the fantastic qualities they embody, Cerezita and Skriker can also be thought within Donna Haraway's conception of a "cyborg" as nonhuman species which coexist with human beings (135–158) In her comprehensive essay "Manifesto for Cyborgs: Science, Technology, and Socialist-Feminism in the 1980s", Haraway chooses to describe the cyborg through the term "affinity" as an alternative to the term identity which inevitably implies "ideologies of gender, race and class". (149–181) In other words, Haraway urges to think the "cyborg" outside the signifiers of human. Moraga's choice of the word "automated" in her note on Cerezita's wheel-chair (90) and Churchill's conscious use of the word "damaged" to describe Skriker strengthen the parallelism by giving a machinery sense.

Similar to the genderless Skriker, born as a head, Cerezita is hardly given any sexual characteristics. In this respect, Cerezita is reminiscent of the Olympian goddess Athena, who was born from Zeus's head and thus attributed both male and female qualities. Haraway's transhumanist conception of "cyborg" which is seemingly the opposite of Olympian deities, urges for a revisiting of mythology which offers the human and non-human side by side. Drawing on Roland Barthes's suggestion of "transformative" quality of myths (54), cyborg can indeed be read as the transformed version of the old image of the supernatural, non-human living with human. However, the term "cyborg" with its implied context offers less optimism as it signifies a world more mechanized, a life further away from nature.

Undoing the anthropocentric views with unlimited powers of imagination and dramatization, Cherrie Moraga and Caryl Churchill's plays make a call for a possible reconnection with nature. Reflecting their ecofeminist stances as two feminist writers making an urgent call for putting environment on the agenda. In other words, *Heroes and Saints* and *The Skriker* urge for possibilities of rethinking mankind's relation with nature before nature becomes man's antagonist.

Works Cited

Anzaldua, Gloria. *Borderlands: La Frontera. The New Mestiza*. Aunt Luke Books, 1999.

Barthes, Roland. "Myth Today". *Mythologies*. New York: Noonday Press, 1972.

Churchill, Caryl. *The Skriker*. Theatre Communications Group, 1994.

Clark, Timothy. *The Cambridge Introduction to Literature and Environment*. Cambridge: Cambridge UP, 2011.

Gates, Henri Luis. *The Signifying Monkey and a Theory of Afro-American Literary Criticism*. New York, Oxford: Oxford UP, 1988.

Hamilton, Edith. *Mythology: Timeless Tales of Gods and Heroes*. New York; Boston: Grand Central Publishing, 2011.

Harraway, Donna. "Manifesto for Cyborgs: Science, Technology, and Socialist-Feminism in the 1980s." *Australian Feminist Studies*. 2. 4. 1987, 1–42.

Merchant, Carolyn. *The Death of Nature*: *Women, Ecology, and the Scientific Revolution,* 1980

Moraga, Cherrie. *Heroes and Saints &Other Plays*. West End Press, 1986.

Pope, Alexander. "An Essay on Criticism". 1711.

Woolf, Virginia. "Mr. Bennett and Mrs. Brown". http://www.columbia. edu/~em36/MrBennettAndMrsBrown.pdf

Wordsworth, William. *The Complete Poetical Works of William Wordsworth*. Ed. Henry Reed. Philadelphia: Hayes & Zell, 1854.

Nilay Kaya and Ekin Gündüz Özdemirci

Embodied Anthropocentrism in Anatolian Novel and Film

The first discussions of environmental justice in Turkish cultural scene in the early years of Turkish Republic appeared in the late 1950s, under the influence of social realist movement both in literature and film. Drawing upon the subject of 'right to water', *Dry Summer* is one of the first examples in Turkish film and literature that explore the issue of social justice from an environmental justice perspective. In this comparative analysis of the novella and the film we will discuss the treatment of environmental issues in social realist works, and comment on the ethical understanding of non-human nature in a period that is largely unexplored within ecocriticism studies in Turkey.

'Predicament' of Water Shortage

Necati Cumalı's *Dry Summer* has not been studied through an ecological approach so far, yet there has been some mention of its premonition that within years to come water would exceedingly turn into a private property, in parallel with the increase of deforestation and draught.[1] Considering today's extreme global manipulation of water resources in the form of dams, reservoirs, canals or expanded bottled water markets, and the obstructing effects of hydroelectric power plants on natural habitats, which is a highly up-to-date local problem in Turkey, *Dry Summer* deserves to be studied in terms of its plot. But the main question here is how far does *Dry Summer* actually present, predicate or draw attention to an ecological problem "of an entire agricultural village faced with water shortage".

---

1 Ufuk Özdağ points out to the novels, which deal with the environmental problems especially taking place in Anatolian rural life, mentioning Necati Cumalı's *Dry Summer*. See: *The Future of Ecocriticism: New Horizons.* (ed.). Serpil Oppermann, Ufuk Özdağ, Nevin Özkan and Scott Slovic. Newcastle upon Tyne: Cambridge Scholars Publishing, 2011.

Necati Cumalı (1921–2001) is a writer whose thematic concerns are broad but his focusing of the hardships of rural life (mostly West Anatolian lands) stands out in his oeuvre.[2] At first, he intends to give *Dry Summer* the title of "Habil ve Kabil" (Cain and Abel). With this direct ancient reference, he aims to draw attention to the never-ending problem of desire to possess the land and the rivalry between brothers but then he changes the title as *Dry Summer*. The reason behind his decision is unknown but the new title refers to a more environmental problem rather than a basic human conflict and fairly enough it gives way to a direct assumption that the novella's main concern is to point out water shortage on a micro level, choosing an agricultural area as the setting.

Dry Summer takes place in a village of Urla in Western Anatolia, Aegean region, at the end of 1940s and early 1950s. In the beginning of summer Hasan Kocabaş decides to block the spring on his property because that summer would be too dry to support all the farmers who rely on its waters. The farmers resist and get furious with Hasan, ultimately, they start a legal dispute. In the end Hasan wins the case as the law indicates that whoever has the deed of the land gets the right to water. This ignites an apparent rivalry and Hasan kills one of the farmers attacking his land. He convinces his brother Osman to take the blame for the killing as he is much younger and will get a lighter sentence. Hasan exploits this situation to get Osman's wife Bahar who lives in the same house. He destroys Osman's letters to make it appear as if he has forgotten Bahar. When another prisoner named Osman is murdered in the same prison with his brother, Hasan uses this chance to make Bahar believe that her husband is dead and finally achieves his goal of getting her. Osman gets pardoned eventually and he goes directly to confront his brother. When two brothers are about to fire their guns and shoot each other, Bahar appears with a rifle unexpectedly and shoots Hasan to death.

---

2   His work is mainly classified as "Anatolian village novels" subgenre in social realist Turkish literature which was dominant in between 1950s and 1970s. Anatolian novels, some of them called "village novels", mainly focus on the problem of land as property; social justice, the conflicts between farmers and landowners, workers and factory owners, illiteracy and education; migration from rural areas to the cities, often within Marxist approach.

Water Conflicts and Civil Violence

In the plot, the rivalry between humans stands out as the main dramatic conflict most clearly, not the water problem itself. Considering the historical background, it is a fact that Western Anatolia, mainly the Aegean region was always fertile and for this very reason, land control has always led to severe civil violence apart from the wars. When *Dry Summer* was written and published, Aegan region had the highest rates in agricultural production especially between 1950s and 1960s.[3] This may be a reason that the relations of property reveal themselves as more strained, intense and harsh as the plot of the novella exemplifies. Hasan's main motivation for blocking the spring on his property seems to be his worrying about the upcoming draught at first, but in the beginning of the novella we also come across this sentence: "This water was going to make him rich. [...] In a few years they would drop off *loads*[4] of apricots and peaches in the market place." (Cumalı 11) Hasan's actual motivation appears as possessing more than a basic survival problem depending upon the lands: he wants to become rich, he wants to harvest and sell loads of products. The constant repetitions in the narration, reflecting directly his mind reveal the attitude of perceiving the natural resource as property: "Water is coming from his own land. Surely he wasn't rich enough to distribute it lavishly!" From the beginning to the end we witness an paramount desire for possession in his attitude and almost immediate violent reactions caused by the tension of controlling the water, in other words, power.

On a macro level, "Life support systems changes can shake societies. A rich archive of historic evidence shows how water scarcity and deterioration of water quality has contributed to the decline of ancient empires." (Falkenmark, Wang-Erlandsson and Rockström 9) The Pacific Institute thinktank which has been tracking a database of events related to water and conflict from 3000 BC to this day defines the forms of conflict and presents water "as a trigger or root cause of conflict, where there is a dispute over the control of water or water systems or where economic or

---

3   For the statistics see Yavuz, Fahri. *Türkiye'de Tarım* (Agriculture in Turkey). Tarım ve Köy İşleri Bakanlığı: Aralık 2005.
4   Italics belong to the writers of the article.

physical access to water, or scarcity of water."[5] *Dry Summer* stands out as the example of this definition on a micro level with a local focus: The water shortage and blocking the spring can be considered as the triggering action in the plot and this rising action initiates immediately a certain type of violence that is spread throughout the novella at an increasing rate. But even before the rising action, namely Hasan's act, in the introduction part of the story, we observe the inclination to a collective violence due to water problem. As summer proceeds, the temper of the farmers who check the height of the water in the pool changes:

> The shorter the water gets, the higher the impatience and anger of the men grow. It becomes possible to see them catching kids, who play by the water, in order to beat and chase them; sometimes they get in a fight with the herdsmen who want to water their herds a little. Very often, squabbles arise between the neighbours who attempt to turn the direction of the water to their yards. But all this hubbub blows over when the first signs of rain appear in the sky. (Cumalı 9)

This delicate tension, so to speak, haunts all the villagers leading to amplified conflicts, shaking the social order of the village. After Hasan's action, the children who are unjustly treated and violated by the grown-ups in the quote above, respond with physical violence, too. They throw stones at Osman, even though they see him as a much milder and nicer person than Hasan and know that he does not support his older brother's decision. We witness the acceleration of the collective rage and its possible consequences as "[t]he hostility of the neighbors, in the emptiness caused by the lack of this sound lies in ambush; waiting for the day of revenge, getting bigger and bigger." (Cumalı 25)

The Silenced Water

It should be emphasized that in the novella there is neither a single implication of a drastic problem of water shortage and drought showing itself year by year, nor a common concern mutually shared by the characters. But far more importantly, the anthropocentric attitude is embedded in the narrative mood per se. Omitting the inherent being of non-human nature,

---

5   Pacific Institute. "Water Conflict Chronology". Pacific Institute, Oakland, CA. (2019). https://www.worldwater.org/water-conflict/. Accessed: (25.05.20).

mainly water, reverberates in using it as a literary tool, in its imagery, mostly visible in the descriptions. The first depiction of water appears quite functional in terms of expressing its physical condition and effect on humans' lands:

> [w]hen the summer comes, two of the three springs that water the lands lying in slight waves get dry; [...] Then, in that region, until the first autumnal raindrops fall, just one single sound of water is heard. In Tekebaşı, a water vein thick as a bicep bubbling from the skirts of the small olive grove of Kocabaş family, in its one fathom in length bed, at first swells quickly, overflows; then through a stone gutter partially plastered with mortar, begins to flow into a pool five or six paces below. (Cumalı 7)

A portrayal of natural environment, presenting its inherent existence, does not have to be idyllic nor sound like Romantic poetry necessarily. However, this portrayal requires to be observed by asking the question, "for whom water is valuable?" "Value is an indication of how something is assessed qualitatively or quantitatively, and it is a term for what should be retained or realized." (Havsteen-Mikkelsen 16) In the description quoted above, water is depicted through its physical condition as the element of nutrition. Shortly after the first sentences, the narrative angle penetrates a private estate and reveals its path throughout the novella more clearly: towards human. And the answer to the question, "for is whom water valuable?" becomes obvious. As the story proceeds, water takes part only on the condition that a human will be portrayed, without exception. It does not stand as an entity nor a character but a subsidiary literary tool, functioning in telling the human condition.

The sound of water in a repetitive way can be used as a poetic enforcement in a narrative and this may serve to crystallize the entity of water itself. Yet, in the case of *Dry Summer*, the water sounds 'sound' for the sake of humans eminently. If we look at the examples where water seemingly sounds, we actually witness its silence.[6] Hasan listens to the sound of water at nights which becomes an efficient leitmotif in the narrative in order

---

6   Christopher Manes claims that in our world, non-human nature is actually silent and "the status that being a speaking subject is jealously guarded as an exclusively human prerogative." See: Manes, Christopher. "Nature and Silence", *Environmental Ethics* 14–4 (1992). 339–50.

to build the mood and motivation of a character: "When the breathings
inside ceased, he used to listen to the water. The sound of water calmed
Hasan Kocabaş, it told him stories, drifted him to dreams, and yet left him
sleepless." (Cumalı 11) Hasan even takes an erotic pleasure from hearing
the sound of water filling the private pool that he made, as he eavesdrops
on his brother and his wife's making love next door; as the breaths of the
couple are distinctly accompanied by the sounds of water. In a similar
way, in the portrayal of Hasan's neighbor and rival Veli, once again, we
come across the use of non-human nature sounds that are in the service
of characterization and the mood, in the very name of telling "the human
condition". His realizing the absence of sound is emphasized and "the
golden sound which made him sleep with ease" (Cumalı 13) terrifies him.
The sounds of water act in disguise of its "own" language as the value of
it is directed to human concerns. Metaphorically speaking, as long as the
pool of humans is filled with water, the sound of it is muted because its
value is determined by and for humans; showing how the novella's attitude
is aligned with the Anthropocene discourse.

Visualizing *Dry Summer*

The film adaptation of *Dry Summer* has been groundbreaking in the development of modern Turkish cinema with its realist exploration of human
conditions in rural life, innovative poetic film aesthetic and international
success in film festivals. Along with *The Revenge of the Snakes* (1962)
and *The Well* (1968), *Dry Summer* (1964) is one of the three prominent
rural films of director Metin Erksan, often credited as his "ownership
trilogy" due to the films' rights-based stories, respectively on the possession of land, water and woman. While adapting the novella to film Metin
Erksan was influenced by the period's social realist movement in cinema
that was inspired by Italian post-war neo-realism and socially realistic
village novels that became widespread in Turkey from 1950s.[7] The film

7   Until the end of 1950s the greater part of the population was still living in rural
    areas in Turkey and their stories were not foregrounded in a realist manner
    within the rush of nationalist films targeting the modernization ideals of the
    young Turkish Republic or in escapist melodramas with idyllic rural settings.
    Some prominent examples of rural films either adapted or influenced from village

adaptation maintains the core story, but improves some elements such as the critique of patriarchy and the discourse of environmental justice. A significant difference is a switch in names, Osman is the elder and Hasan is the younger brother in the film in contrast to the novella.[8]

Osman's prominent greed of ownership is linked to his oppressive masculinity and sexuality and frames the film's narrative. In the first half of the film, the story is shaped by his struggle to have control over water, and the second half is about his desire to possess and dominate Bahar.

Non-human Nature as the 'other'

Dry Summer starts with scenes that display the villagers who mix their labor with the natural environment. In the opening scenes we see Osman on a donkey and another one next to him carrying stuff, moving ahead on the narrow streets of the village. That is followed by the images of villagers working on their land, hoeing the soil. These people's livelihood depends on the natural environment where they live in, besides, the affinity between labor and nature is determinant on their course of life. In two scenes the characters talk about how getting married - which is a vital moral value in a patriarchal society – depends on the harvest time of crops. In an early scene where Hasan and Bahar meet secretly as they are not married yet, Hasan insists on getting married soon and Bahar reminds that her mother would only give the permission after the harvest time. In the second half of the film, after Hasan is put in jail, Osman makes a similar statement when Bahar asks him to find someone to marry because of the increasing social pressure on her for living under the same roof with a widower.

---

novels in early Turkish cinema are: Lütfi Ö. Akad's *White Handkerchief (Beyaz Mendil, 1955)* adapted from internationally acclaimed writer Yaşar Kemal's story; Atıf Yılmaz's *The Girl Who Guarded The Mountains (Dağları Bekleyen Kız, 1955)* adapted from Esat Mahmut Karakurt's novel; Nedim Otyam's *Land (Toprak, 1952)*; Metin Erksan's *Dark World (Karanlık Dünya, 1952)*; Lütfi Ö. Akad's Anatolian trilogy: *The Law of Border (Hudutların Kanunu, 1967)*, *Kızılırmak Karakoyun (1967)* and *River (Irmak, 1972)*.

8   There are opinions stating that Erksan named the good-natured character Hasan after the prophet Muhammad's grandson, yet the real motivation behind this modification remains unknown.

Despite these references of their living intertwined with the natural environment, the villagers' priorities and values, as well as the film's approach
to natural environment remain anthropocentric. In visual terms, the film
lacks a 'more-than-human' perspective; regarding screen time and number
of close up scenes, natural environment doesn't take place as an inclusive
filmic character, it lacks agency.[9] Independent scenes of non-human nature
are limited with screen times varying between two to five seconds before
eventually human characters enter the frame. This human-centered perspective is maintained in the film's discourse of environmental justice. Even
though the film interrogates the issue of 'nature as property' the argument
of justice remains limited as the environmental problems are not identified and non-human nature is reduced into resources in equal service for
human concerns. The film does not foreground any shifting environmental
factor that encourages Osman to block the water unlike he did in the previous years. There is not an emphasis on an ecological risk or problem
besides two scenes with two statements on a possible drought and the risk
of water scarcity in near future due to the rise in population. The main
motive of Osman to control the water is presented as the expansion of his
cultivated land. Water is a resource for his ends and his right to it comes
with his property. The villagers don't differ from Osman in moral values;
they remain silent when he asks them if they would not react the same way
if they had the water resource in their own property. This manifests the
mutual moral understanding of nature as a profitable commodity, a source
of livelihood alone and the instrumental value attributed to it.

---

9 We can observe the independent and prominent presence of natural environment in some Turkish art house films produced after 1990s, the period that is
   referred as New Turkish Cinema (Suner, 2010; Dönmez-Colin, 2003; Kaim,
   2011). Contemporary directors such as Reha Erdem, Semih Kaplanoğlu and
   Nuri Bilge Ceylan mainly engage with rural narratives in some of their films,
   where we observe an attempt to capture the wildness of natural environment,
   include it in the flow of the story and create a non-hierarchical bond between
   human and non-human nature. For a wider ecocritical exploration of New
   Turkish Cinema see: Özdemirci, E. G. "Moving Stills: The Idea of Nature in
   New Turkish Cinema", *Transforming Socio-Natures in Turkey-Landscapes,
   State and Environmental Movements*, Ethemcan Turhan, Onur Inal (Ed.),
   London: Routledge, 2019, 187–207.

The villagers' instrumental approach to non-human nature becomes apparent as they kill Osman's dog Karabaş with a shotgun as a warning to him; killing an animal is a justifiable act for their cause and search for justice. This is the only scene where we see the dog; the animal has a name but no real presence in the film, remains as a means to display the rising tension and violence among men. The film's critical approach about taking nature as a commodity that can be owned or exploited does not stand out in filmic representation as non-human living beings do not have agency, even worse, this attitude manifests itself in the film's shooting as well.

The film's anthropocentric discourse seems to be in line with the production process. In the scenes where we see the murder of the dog and slaughter of a chicken, it is obvious that animal welfare was not on the agenda during the shooting; even though we can't reach the confirmed data, these acts of violence seem to be practiced in real on animals. There weren't any legal regulations about animal safety in film shootings until The Animal Protection Law (No: 5199)[10] enacted in 2004, which offered animals wider protection and rights, including regulations on animal actors, which interdict the damaging and distressing use of animals in works such as film shootings and spectacles.[11]

There are two relational aspects of environmental ethics: "the justice of the distribution of environments among people, and the justice of the relationship between humans and the rest of the natural world" (Stevis 63). Ignoring the latter in favor of the former and an emphasis on just distribution of natural resources in environmental justice arguments is considered to be an 'ethical exclusion' from an ecocentric perspective (Stevis, 2000;

---

10 By year of 2020 a more comprehensive draft law under the name of the Animal Rights Law, which changes the status of animals and accepts them as partly legal subjects, thus aiming to prevent violation of rights in addition to protection, is presently under discussion in parliamentary commissions.

11 As there isn't an official monitoring commission to secure the fair application of this law, in 2018 HAYTAP (Hayvan Hakları Federasyonu – Animal Rights Federation) declared that they established a voluntary observer service to monitor film shootings. The declaration of HAYTAP, reports on observations from film sets and related media coverage can be examined on the NGO's official website: https://www.haytap.org/index.php/tv-dizileri-ve-filmlerinde-haytap/ haytap-sanat-hayvanlarin-kullanildigi-film-sektorunde-haytap-denetimi

Plumwood, 2003; Temper, 2018). That leads to a distinction between environmental and ecological justice, which is, unlike the former, inclusive of the 'rights of nature' and relatedly the consideration of ecological obligations and consequences of actions. Regarding this, the discourse of 'right to water' remains as a human-centered social justice issue and a shallow environmental justice argument in *Dry Summer*. Instead of an ethical stance that is based on a discourse of responsibility, we observe a one-sided right-based discourse giving non-human nature an instrumental and secondary place.

Patriarchy and the 'greed of ownership'

Expanding the human-centered ethics of environmental justice requires the criticism of anthropocentrism and its foundations of dualistic thinking and human-supremacy. Val Plumwood defines the main logic of these foundations as moral dualism:

> Moral dualism makes an emphatic division of the world into two starkly contrasting orders, consisting of those privileged beings considered subject to full-blown ethical concern as 'humans' or 'persons', and the remainder, considered beneath ethical concern and belonging to an instrumental realm of resources (or, in the prevailing political context, of 'property') available to the first group. (Plumwood 191)

Osman's 'greed of ownership' is representative of humankind's power struggle over non-human nature, as well as within its own species in the current Anthropocene era. Supremacy is a form of 'othering', and when we talk about the bond between anthropocentrism and human-supremacy in the context of human's relation to the non-human world, that also includes humankind's attitude of supremacy within its own species based on race, gender or economic class. As Alvin Y. Wang states: "The ideology, which authorizes oppressions such as those based on race, class, gender, sexuality, physical abilities and species is the same ideology which sanctions the oppression of nature" (Wang 2411). And this reveals how anthropocentrism is interconnected with socioeconomic power and ego dynamics. The way Erksan frames the issue of property around the critic of patriarchy and argument of environmental justice opens space for the interrogation of these complex interrelations.

In *Water and Dreams* (1999) Gaston Bachelard depicts water as a feminine element and defines it as an eye that is the originary mirror. Along with Bahar, water is the object of Osman's desire and reflective of his greed. In that sense, the film depicts two objects of desire of the patriarchy in parallel, water as a natural resource and the female existence. As in the myth of Narcissus who was blind to look beyond his own reflection on water, Osman is blind to see beyond his illusion of power, which is identified with his androcentrism and possession of water resource. At the end of the film, just like Narcissus, Osman's blind desire and illusion carry him to death as he dies in water after a greedy fight with his brother and his corpse is drifted with the current.

As Karen Warren states, anthropocentrism has historically functioned as androcentrism, which is structured around male dominance hierarchies (Warren, 1999, 257). Hierarchical relationships where one exercises power over another; the 'power-over' conceptions of power (Warren, 2000, 46) in Warren's terms, are foregrounded in the film to reflect the patriarchal oppression as a social agreement. Throughout the film Osman uses the advantage of being the elder brother in a patriarchal family structure. Hasan gently states his opinions but never goes against Osman stating that "you are my elder, you know better", and even unwillingly falls in line with all his decisions. As Bahar joins the family after the marriage she also adopts the same attitude and statements towards Osman.

Osman, as the figure of patriarchal power, is portrayed as a self-seeking villain character. He is often captured in extreme low-angle-shots, which are taken from below eye level and create a sense of strength, power and pressure concerning the subject. On several occasions, the camera shows Osman looking down on Bahar and Hasan, and sometimes his legs dominate the background of Hasan's close up face shots during their dialogue scenes. The only scenes where we see Osman from above eye level display him getting physically close to Bahar, revealing his weakness owing to his lust for her.

Multiple scenes of Osman's aggressive behavior and exaggerated erotic gestures towards Bahar, such as watching her as he drinks milk from the cow's udder, unveil the nature of his androcentric and patriarchal hunger for power. Right after he achieves his goal to sleep with her, we see him having Bahar wash his feet as a display of his 'power-over' power.

According to Warren, the conceptual framework of patriarchy is based on value-hierarchical thinking, which is "giving higher status to what has been traditionally identified as 'male' than to what has been traditionally identified as 'female', and this framework gives rise to a logic of domination, which serves to legitimate inequality (Chakraborty 126). In the first night of their wedding as Hasan and Bahar are in their room making love, we witness Osman's brutal attack on their private space. The scene is hyperbolic and absurd with Osman's grotesque act of breaking the windows and diving into their bedroom as he is drunk, commanding the couple to make lots of children by screaming: "I want baby boys! They will be men just like me!" The film reveals how woman is reduced into an object of desire or child bearer, and this also applies to non-human nature from a value-hierarchical perspective, which justifies subordination based on the idea of superiority. In an absurd scene, the oppression of woman and non-human intertwine; Osman slaughters a chicken, then he throws the animal's dead body towards Bahar, shouts with a laughter: "It's necessary to frighten the woman-kind time to time."

As explored in the film, the oppression of woman and non-human nature relate to the various forms of domination resulting from the same value-hierarchical thinking based on male bias and chauvinism. Regarding this, Erksan uses the scarecrow on Osman's land as an important symbol that underscores both androcentrism and anthropocentrism in the film narrative. It reflects Osman's position of power and becomes the witness of his greed. He uses the gun he hides in the scarecrow's pocket while running away from the villagers who demand their right to water, putting the scarecrow in place of Bahar, he rehearses a speech and abusively flirts with it, and uses it as a target during his training to kill his younger brother Hasan. When Bahar finds out about Hasan's death, with the first shock of the traumatic news she runs to hug the scarecrow, crying and screaming. Spinning camera reflects her whole world turning upside down, and displays her imperative surrender to the remaining male power in the patriarchal family.

The scarecrow can be described as the symbol of property; it is only placed in a land that is owned, and it is often designed as a male figure. At the same time, as being a tool for keeping animals away from the harvest, it is a way of human intervention in nature. As a manlike figure the scarecrow protects the manufactured lands and becomes a symbolic object of man's oppressive struggle with the human and non-human 'others.'

The film achieves to elicit a critical discussion of patriarchy and explore the common oppression of women and non-human nature in an androcentric context. The environmental justice argument in this discussion however, relies on a "conception of nature as a passive object that can be more justly and evenhandedly distributed among human populations through different property rights, allocations, etc." (Temper 13). Such a rights-based perspective justifies a one-sided relationship with non-human nature that is based on human's equal access to its resources, and reinforces the value-hierarchical thinking.

Anthropocentrism Unfolded

Considering the two narratives, although both plots are based on the issue of 'right to water', the emphasis is not on an environmental problem such as the risk of draught or water scarcity in near future. So, the assumption that both the novella and the film have a predicative attitude towards the ecological condition fails to a certain degree. In any case, water conflicts result in a degraded human security, loss of rules of law, amplified conflicts both in the nuclear family and within the village people, and lastly homicide. Nonetheless the emphasis on the representation of social conditions, and 'human conditions' in particular, leaves not much room for the consideration of an inherent meaning and an independent presence of the non-human nature. Both in the novella and the film, human attitude towards non-human nature is based on its instrumental usefulness for human concerns and purposes, not only contextually but also in form, acting as an agency in the service of representing the human.

The film adaptation emphasizes the issue of environmental justice in a more prominent way compared to the novella, incorporating clear statements of villagers stressing their objection to the idea of 'nature as property', and many scenes demonstrating the characters' uprising with attempts to unblock the spring, while it takes place only once in the novella. The modified ending of the film also contributes to its emphasis on justice; the younger brother kills the elder one in the water, unblocks the barrier and the water flows freely again along with the corpse of his brother.

Unlike the film, Cumalı doesn't mention the unblocking in the end of the novella and concludes the story with the murder Bahar commits. Erksan ends the film with an androcentric power and moral struggle and the male heroic act of killing, which points to the ongoing domination of patriarchal values. In the novella Bahar remains inactive and silent until she kills Osman in the end. Presumably inspired from this insurgent act, Erksan develops the woman's agency, which shapes and fortifies the film's critique of patriarchal values and their association with anthropocentrism.

Works Cited

Bachelard, Gaston. *Water and Dreams*. Dallas: Pegasus Foundation, 1999.

Chakraborty, Roma. "The Deep Ecology/Ecofeminism Debate: An Enquiry into Environmental Ethics". *Journal of Indian Council of Philosophical Research* 32:1 (2015). 123–133.

Cumalı, Necati. *Susuz Yaz* (Dry Summer). Istanbul: Cumhuriyet Kitapları, 2019.

Dönmez-Colin, Gönül. "New Turkish Cinema – Individual Tales of Common Concerns". *Asian Cinema* 14:1 (2003). 138–145.

Falkenmark, Malin, Lan Wang-Erlandsson and Johan Rockström. "Understanding of Water Resilience in the Anthropocene". *Journal of Hydrology X* 2 (2019). 1–13.

Havsteen-Mikkelsen, Gudrun Eriksen. "Symbiosis of Human and Water in the Anthropocene". Final Thesis for a BA-degree Icelandic Academy of the Arts Department of Design and Architecture. December 2016.

Kaim, Agnieszka A. "New Turkish Cinema – Some Remarks on the Homesickness of the Turkish Soul". *Cinej Cinema Journal*, Special Issue 1 (2011). 99–106.

Manes, Christopher. "Nature and Silence", *Environmental Ethics* 14–4 (1992). 339–50.

Özdemirci, Ekin G. "Moving Stills: The Idea of Nature in New Turkish Cinema". *Transforming Socio-Natures in Turkey-Landscapes, State and Environmental Movements*. (ed.). Ethemcan Turhan, Onur Inal. London: Routledge, 2019, 187–207.

Pacific Institute. "Water Conflict Chronology". Pacific Institute, Oakland, CA. (2019). https://www.worldwater.org/water-conflict/. Accessed: 25.05.20.

Plumwood, Val. "Ecological Ethics from Rights to Recognition: Multiple Spheres of Justice for Humans, Animals and Nature". *Global Ethics and Environment.* (ed.). Nicholas Law. New York: Routledge, (2003). 188–212.

Stevis, Dimitris. "Whose Ecological Justice?". *Strategies* 13:1 (2000). 63–76.

Suner, Asuman. *New Turkish Cinema: Belonging, Identity and Memory.* New York: I. B. Tauris, 2010.

Temper, Leah. "Blocking Pipelines, Unsettling Environmental Justice: From Rights of Nature to Responsibility to Territory." *Local Environment, The International Journal of Justice and Sustainability.* (2018). 1–19. DOI: 10.1080/13549839.2018.1536698.

Opperman, Serpil et all (eds.). *The Future of Ecocriticism: New Horizons.* (ed.). Serpil Oppermann, Ufuk Özdağ, Nevin Özkan and Scott Slovic. Newcastle upon Tyne: Cambridge Scholars Publishing, 2011.

Wang, Alvin Y. "Gender and Nature: A Psychological Analysis of Ecofeminist Theory". *Journal of Applied Social Psychology* 29:11 (1999). 2410–2424.

Warren, Karen J. "Ecofeminist Philosophy and Deep Ecology". *Philosophical Dialogues: Arne Naess and the Progress of Ecophilosophy.* (ed.). Nina Witoszek, Andrew Brennan. Oxford: Rowman & Littlefield Publishers, 1999. 255–269.

Warren, Karen J. *Ecofeminist Philosophy: A Western Perspective on What It Is and Why It Matters.* Rowman & Littlefield, 2000.

Yavuz, Fahri. *Türkiye'de Tarım* (Agriculture in Turkey). Tarım ve Köy İşleri Bakanlığı: Aralık 2005.

Burcu Kayışcı Akkoyun

Intersections, Interventions, and Utopian Pessimism in *Son Ada (The Last Island)*

To begin with a fitting metaphor for this essay, the first seeds were planted in the early summer of 2019 during a time when the Turkish State Meteorological Service was issuing flood warnings due to heavy rainfall, and the third anniversary of the July 15 coup attempt in Turkey was just around the corner. These seemingly unrelated events took on a new meaning in light of the novel I was working on at the time: *Son Ada (The Last Island)* by Zülfü Livaneli (2008), which portrays the short-sighted policies of a retired general/newly turned President, and the ensuing catastrophic transformation of a fictional island from a eutopia[1] into a dystopia. The novel is available only in Turkish at present, and yet, this essay is an attempt to demonstrate that Livaneli not only problematizes but also aims to transcend a sense of closure within national borders through his intersectional critique of authoritarian and anthropocentric perceptions that simultaneously threaten the lives of human and non-human residents of the earth. The trajectory of this double operation, I argue, could be explored both in the intertextual space in which the author gestures towards different literary genres, and the conventions of Western utopian/dystopian fiction, and in the temporality of the narrative that oscillates between the past, the present, and the future, endorsing an environmental ethos. My reading takes its cue from the oft-quoted first rule of ecology formulated by the American biologist and ecologist Barry Commoner: "Everything is connected to everything else" (35). It is thus vital to observe the fine balance of this interconnectedness in nature, which is in fact not isolated from cultural and political dynamics of human communities.

Utopian/dystopian visions articulated in philosophy, politics, and literature have been particularly useful to address the deep-seated questions concerning happiness, freedom, equality and progress, and to situate humans

---

1   I use *eutopia*, the homophone of *utopia*, in parts where I want to shift the stress from "imaginary (no) place" to "good place."

-sometimes self-righteously and sometimes critically at the center- within their surroundings. Insofar as it is considered primarily a Western cultural product, whether an autonomous utopian tradition exists in Turkish literature has been debated by scholars especially in the last decades due to the growing interest in utopian and dystopian fiction. Despite differing opinions, researchers agree that utopian thought has operated and produced narratives in tandem with the modernization process that began in the 19th century. During the First and the Second Constitutional Eras (1876 and 1908), intellectuals of the time contemplated on the reasons for the decline of the Ottoman Empire and envisioned socially, politically and culturally better alternatives. The modernization or "Westernization" attempts gained momentum after Mustafa Kemal Atatürk founded the Turkish Republic in 1923. It is thus no coincidence that many works embodying utopian visions were created particularly in the first half of the 20th century even though utopia is rarely, if not never, considered a full-fledged genre that presents new aesthetic possibilities in Turkish literature. While the first decades of the Turkish Republic retained the utopian spirit and perhaps even realized its own eutopia thanks to the ongoing Kemalist reforms, the second half of the 20th century revealed a dark, dystopian vein in the literary responses to socio-political issues. These issues stemmed largely from the conflicts between deep-rooted traditional/cultural codes and progressive movements in the nation-building process. Fiction of the time depicted the urban-rural dichotomy, alienation of the intelligentsia, power relations in family life and relationships, and the traumas caused by political oppression and escalating militarism. The military coups that have been haunting Turkish history and inhibiting the growth of a democratic culture since the 60s even lead to the formation of a distinct literary genre that reflects in a dystopian manner their impact on individuals' psyche. *Son Ada* could also be included in the body of this "witness literature" in its portrayal of an ex-military President who is all too familiar to the Turkish readers. In his foreword to the novel, Yaşar Kemal, who is arguably the greatest novelist in Turkish literature, compares Livaneli's work to the dictator novels, which emerged in reaction to the rapaciousness of one-man regimes in Latin America. Kemal rightly praises *Son Ada* for its unique treatment of authoritarianism, power and resistance. Still, it could be suggested that the novel derives its critical power more from the thematic and formal dialogue between the national post-military "coup novels," Latin American dictator novels, and utopian/dystopian writing than from a single-handed treatment of a global phenomenon. At this point, Magali Armillas-Tiseyra's views on dictator novels correspond to my understanding of Livaneli's novel. Dictator novels, she observes, both "share critical and formal conventions that make it possible to identify them as a group" and "borrow from other textual and narrative sources, which vary depending on the political context and literary-historical moment of production" (9). Without succumbing to generic labels, as any proficient author would do, Livaneli builds hermeneutic bridges between literary texts and socio-political contexts, and explores formal interactions. But the significance of the novel lies in that it also recognizes the agency of non-humans, or more-than humans, through what I call, to adapt from Mikhail Bakhtin, an environmental chronotope (time-space).[2] This designation offers an expansion, rather than a subversion, of Bakhtin's critical lens that scrutinizes novelistic narratives mainly to illuminate the ideological relationships between human agents and larger social structures as well as the labor aspect and modes of production inside and outside the texts.

Son Ada opens with a metonymic sentence encapsulating the course of the story: "We had been living peacefully in this heaven on earth, which we call 'the best kept secret,' until one day 'he' showed up"[3] (15). Livaneli integrates the Arcadian myth into another predominantly Western form that is island utopia. Imaginary islands have been oft-visited literary tropes since the ancient times, and it is perhaps no coincidence that utopia as a distinct literary genre is named after the eponymous island Thomas More envisioned in 1516. The last island is described by the unnamed narrator as a beautiful idyllic place far from all mainlands as typical of all Arcadian spaces. It is surrounded by a crystal-clear sea and covered with pine trees. The weather is always mild, and the night breeze carries the fragrance

---

2   In his essay "Forms of Time and of the Chronotope in the Novel: Notes toward a Historical Poetics," Bakhtin defines chronotope as "the intrinsic connectedness of temporal and spatial relationships that are artistically expressed in literature" (84).

3   All translations from the novel are mine.

of the jasmines throughout the year. Here, seagulls are "the most important neighbours" of the inhabitants and "the real owners of the island" (19). When a wealthy businessperson bought the island many years ago to spend his old age, he also encouraged his friends and acquaintances to build houses next to his mansion and ease his loneliness. He did not ask for money, and people used extra resources at the minimum to complete the collective construction process in total harmony with nature. After forty houses were built, the man, who is referred to as Number 1, stopped the process not to damage the island's habitat. Although the readers are not provided with a detailed social plan concerning the organization of social and political life in the strict sense of classical utopias, the narrator explains that the necessary goods are transported by a ferry every week, and the grocery store near the dock sells these items. The islanders -again collectively- pick and sell pine nuts as a major source of income. Despite this seemingly peaceful atmosphere, the narrator simultaneously laments that happy days are over, and things will never be the same again. Peace on the island is disrupted by the arrival of an outsider. These passages not only expand on the laconic opening sentence of the novel but also reveal the narrator's deep sense of remorse caused by the failure to take responsibility and action when necessary.

In his extensive work on the representation of islands in English literature, Akşit Göktürk observes that human imagination is inclined to conceive islands as atemporal heavenly places away from the challenges of the fast-paced external world (12–13). Elaborating on the implications of the island image in human psyche and literature, Gilles Deleuze makes a similar point by stating that "Dreaming of islands [...] is dreaming of pulling away, of being already separate, far from any continent, of being lost and alone – or it is dreaming of starting from scratch, recreating, beginning anew" (9). The dwellers of the last island seem to seek both: being away and starting afresh; for some of the characters, it represents a second or a last chance. At first glance, the novel's spatiotemporal structure is reminiscent of Bakhtin's delineation of the "idyllic chronotope" with its (almost) self-sufficient setting organized around the organic unity of time and place, and the attunement of the characters to this unity (225). By turning the dream into a nightmare, however, Livaneli problematizes the conception of an escapist idyllic utopia that disregards ethical/political responsibilities or, as the story later discloses, still condones the very same wrongdoings which are the *raison d'être* of such a venture in the first place. People's initial harmonious coexistence with nature then loses its ethical dimension, failing to maintain an environmentally conscious position in the face of an unexpected intervention that can easily change the course of events for the worse.

Livaneli's critique is conveyed in the story through the arrival of Başkan (The President) following his dismissal by the coup council, which disrupts social harmony on the island as the locals gradually turn into the President's satellites without questioning his purportedly democratic actions. These actions are only nominally democratic insofar as even though the President shares and discusses them with the rest, he manipulates the decision process in line with his own priorities as the self-appointed representative of public opinion and the guardian of social order. At this point, that the inhabitants call each other by their house numbers instead of names could be interpreted in a different –and perhaps more dystopian- light, insinuating the lack of individual identity/integrity as well as of collective resistance against oppression and injustice. Determined to "civilize" the islanders, the President manages to influence the majority with his authoritarian discourse from the very first day. According to the narrator, he has "the airs of a conqueror who has just set foot on the continent of America and seen the half-naked natives" (27). This top-down "civilization" endeavor clearly pertains to Turkish history, but the narrator's analogy between the moment the President sets foot on the island and the origins of the imperialist enterprise indicates that Livaneli addresses the entire history of the world, which is marked with discriminatory and unethical practices towards what is designated and subordinated as the Other. Nature must be subdued, private property rights be reinstated, and resistance be crushed in order to make subjects "civilized." These are the major steps of the colonialist civilizing process that occurs at the expense of those who are deprived of the social and political rights unlike the power holders for whom these rights are "naturally" given, that is, taken for granted in the first place. Turkey may not have an imperial/colonial history itself, and yet the viewpoint represented by the President is an extension of that mentality. Similarly, the island is no more, if not never, the "best kept secret" cut off from the mainland, but rather becomes, in a dystopian manner, yet another *topos* that fails to exceed dualistic modes of thinking.

The binary formulation of culture and nature, which has long been coded as the opposition between civilization and barbarity, or progress and backwardness, in Western imagination has detrimental repercussions not only for the human others that are excluded from the power mechanisms but also for all non-human others that are positioned outside the scope of civilization. In order to analyze this entangled predicament, Val Plumwood employs the concept of "hegemonic centrism," which she describes as "a primary-secondary pattern of attribution that sets up one term (the One) as primary or as centre and defines marginal Others as secondary or derivative in relation to it, for example, as deficient in relation to the centre" (110). "Dominant western culture," she claims, "is androcentric, eurocentric and ethnocentric, as well as anthropocentric." All these hegemonic positions are related to each other in their exclusion, subjugation, and even destruction of what they consider rationally "deficient" such as women, colonial subjects, non-Europeans and non-humans (110). Extending the borders of oppression and exploitation beyond specific locales, Helen Tiffin and Graham Huggan identify a similar connection between anthropocentrism and imperialism by arguing that "assuming a natural prioritisation of humans and human interests over those of other species on earth" is in fact a repetition of "the racist ideologies of imperialism on a planetary scale" (6). Livaneli's literary engagement with the combined damages of androcentrism and anthropocentrism, which finds its expression in an authoritarian militaristic figure, would thus be an appropriate response to the issues that should be approached from an intersectional perspective due to their complex interdependence.

It is remarkable that the first action of the President's men is to cut the trees that lie on one of the main paths, which obliges the islanders to walk under the sun. Upon hearing that there have been prior objections to his self-justified actions, the President decides to form an administrative committee to handle matters "democratically" and reach a consensus. The problem of this decision-making mechanism is that most locals -except for the narrator, his partner Lara, and their close friend, the Author- accept everything the President proposes as if they are stupefied. He has different strategies to intimidate the people and eventually gain their consent.

Once most of the trees are cut, and the rest trimmed to give a sense of order to what he describes as the previously chaotic state of the main path, the President makes a vehement speech that underlines the importance of living in a "civilized" environment as noble human beings. "As you have been living here for a long time," he tells the only three people who have voted against the proposal, "you get used to the disorder and chaos happening under your eyes. Nevertheless, human communities cannot live like this. Civilization necessitates that you put both your lives and your dwellings in order" (41). However, the President's utopian vision of progress does contain more than a touch of civilization on the native trees of the island. His close friendship with Number 1, who is now the first owner's son, opens the latter's eye to the financial investment opportunities and leads him to "kindly" remind the islanders that they actually live on his own property. The locals, for the first time, experience the fear of expulsion from the land they call their own.

The President seeks to exploit the touristic potential of the island by convincing the others that they can get their shares from billion dollars profit if this earthy paradise is adorned with luxury hotels, casinos, and entertainment centers to be constructed by national and global companies. Unlike the narrator, who believes that the seagulls are the real owners of the island and cherished neighbors, he complains that they are a nuisance that prevents people from leaving their uncivilized ways due to the pointless attention they pay for the birds' wellbeing and "the environmentalist nonsense stuffed into [their] heads" (75). The President's attitude perfectly illustrates the "natural prioritisation of humans and human interests" highlighted by Tiffin and Huggan. He explicitly states that "no civilized person would act like this and disregard their own benefit" (75). The precondition of progress, that is, of leaving barbarism behind is putting human-selves at the center and benefiting from a free market economy as well as from rules, regulations and private property. Dominating nature and its non-human inhabitants, by the same token, is a *sine qua non* of building a civilized community for the President since it is the sum of "the methods and regimes that separate humans from animals and render the former honourable" in his view (70). Nature as a "hyper-separate lower order lacking continuity with the human" should simply serve human needs in this anthropocentric view, and so the President "stresses those features which make humans different from nature and animals, rather than those they share with them, as constitutive of a truly human identity" as pointed out by Plumwood (107). This faulty logic reaches its extreme when he invites all on the island to exterminate the seagull population. The obedience of the voters in turn consolidates the power of the President and initiates the catastrophic war waged against the so-called terrorists and nature itself. Anyone who refuses to be a part of the hegemonic system, even the indifferent seagulls whose night walks on rooftops are mistaken for a terrorist attack by the President's men, is now conveniently considered a terrorist.

In her comparative study on dystopian works in the East and the West, Erika Gottlieb claimed that the futuristic dimension of Western dystopian fiction, which portrays the protagonists' present as the future of the readers in a cautionary manner, is "conspicuously absent from the dystopian works written under the totalitarian dictatorships of Eastern and Central Europe." The fictional nightmarish visions are in fact "experienced as historical reality" (17). Gottlieb's perhaps controversial, yet thought-provoking, position could help examine Livaneli's narrative devices in engaging with authoritarianism in Turkish political history, especially the President's recourse to a rhetoric on terrorism and anarchy. Upon seeing that the islanders acquiesce in the fight against the seagulls, the Author, who is the most outspoken critic of the President's ideas and the narrator's and Lara's mostly naïve viewpoint, tells the couple that "[...] whatever has happened in the homeland, its smaller version is operating here. The President has found himself a miniature country for his retirement and will play with it. He will bring in all his experience and use all his dirty tactics" (91). The Author has a point: the President's dirty tactics include attacking the seagulls with heavy weapons, using foxes against them after the birds' counter-attacks, and dealing with the growing number of snakes that appear upon the death or disappearance of the seagulls by poisoning them. On a symbolic level, the novel could be interpreted as a political satire, or what Jameson would identify as a "national allegory"[4] of the experienced historical reality and the present socio-political conjuncture

---

4   See Jameson's "Third-World Literature in the Era of Multinational Capitalism."

in Turkey. The fight against these animals alludes to the fights between different power holders, and political polarization that has hampered democracy and even culminated in military coups more than once in Turkish history. The story thus problematizes the secluded paradisiacal island topos by mirroring the atrocities of the homeland. In accordance with Livaneli's endeavor to exceed formal and national boundaries, however, *Son Ada* should be examined within a larger spatial and temporal framework, which opens up a futuristic critical space when understood through the hermeneutics of the environmental parable on the surface of the narrative. In this respect, an "environmental chronotope" could be a fitting designation for the novel's spatiotemporal structure as Livaneli underlines the embeddedness of culture and nature within the narrative's time-space, and counterpoises the impact of human-made ideologies with the major role played by nature and more-than-humans in shaping the actual reality. This is an artistic task which Bakhtin himself seems to credit when he remarks that "the significance of the idyll in the development of the novel is [...] enormous" even if "[i]ts importance as an underlying image has not been understood and appreciated" sufficiently (228). Livaneli compensates for the lack of appreciation and explication observed -and somewhat displayed- by Bakhtin with his spatially and temporally expanded narrative that explores non-human potentialities and agencies in nature.

In contrast to the expectations of the President and his followers, the island turns into a chaotic, uncanny place simply because the natural balance of its ecosystem is disturbed. The first time the narrator and Lara try to prevent the incidents by distributing handouts, they are labelled as terrorists and anarchists. It should be noted that Livaneli juxtaposes Lara, who courageously and empathetically defends the rights of the non-humans on the island (preparing handouts is her idea in the first place) with both the mostly hesitant and silent narrator and the President's wife whom the two visit as a last resort to stop violence against animals. When Lara requests her to talk to the President about the cruel deeds he has initiated, the wife replies that she has heard so many similar pleas before from the wives of the prisoners, the families of those who are sentenced to death, and mothers who look for their lost children. Her response, she tells Lara and the narrator, has always been the same: "My husband is a statesman and I never get involved in his business. He knows what is best for the state whereas I run the household" (103). The intricate relationship between androcentrism and anthropocentrism pointed out by Plumwood within the context of "hegemonic centrism" becomes visible again in the wife's passive obedience to the "Father of the nation-the Saviour" (37) and the patriarchal norms that are destructive to the secondaries of the binary pattern. Like his friends, the Author tries to stop the massacre of the seagulls too, but he is beaten and detained by the President's men. The fatal consequences of this major disturbance in the ecosystem, however, become evident with the appearance of snakes even inside the houses, which urges people, as well as the President, to acknowledge the gravity of the situation. Yet, the solutions accepted by the majority only exacerbate the ongoing destruction and ruin the island for good.

The President orders powerful chemicals to fight against the snakes and control the fox population. Adopting the militaristic rhetoric of his earlier times, he still believes that the fight against the seagulls is just even though it has failed, "and now the fight against snakes will be won with the same determination" despite a few defeatists, or naysayers, who want to break the high spirits of the society (142). In fact, he is not completely incognizant of the potential danger residing in destroying these interdependent species, but when criticized, he simply reminds the rest that all decisions are taken democratically with the majority vote. His next proposal is to go on an equally brutal hunt for the foxes and to "try a new technique together with the islanders whom [he and his men] turn into monsters" (171). Cyanide infused meat pieces are to be placed in the forest since it is difficult to hunt all the foxes. But, the chain of events turns the island into "a death camp" (171), harming and killing all sorts of animals in the area. Some people are poisoned, too, as cyanide contaminates food and water resources. The ecocide reaches its peak when the President asks his men to start a controlled fire to better spot the animals to shoot, which still meets with no objection as the islanders have now directed all their anger and hatred towards the foxes and wilfully participated in this bloodshed to the disappointment of Lara and the narrator. Starting from the pine nut trees that have been feeding the locals, the wooden houses and eventually the whole island burn down. The futuristic dimension and the cautionary potential of this eutopia-turned-dystopia lies in the way Livaneli depicts the long-term consequences of short-sighted and profit-oriented instrumental policies that disregard the balance in nature as well as in socio-political relations. These policies, he warns the readers, culminate in a vicious cycle that operates to the detriment of even those who position themselves at the heart of hegemonic formations.

The environmental chronotope of the narrative, which mediates between various forms, modes, and generic conventions, allows Livaneli to problematize an insular approach to literary products. The author concomitantly underscores the interconnectedness between individuals and species, inviting the readers to contemplate on the implications of authority, evil, consent, and solidarity. In an opinion piece entitled "Dictators in Literature," Livaneli poses the questions that guide his works: "Why does humanity feel the need to find and commit to a dictator regardless of historical and geographical differences? Is it an innate or a learned behaviour? Is it not worth trying to understand this?"("Edebiyatta") *Son Ada*, like any literary text, conveys more than its author's questions or intentions. Therefore, it cannot and should not be "a transparent document of exploitation or a propagandistic blueprint for the liberation of the oppressed" in Tiffin and Huggan's words (14). Still, the philosophical conversations between the Author and the narrator, and the retrospective storytelling of the latter serve Livaneli's purposes of creating a critical space in the literary text and "drawing attention to [...] its capacity to set out symbolic guidelines for the material transformation of the world" without making aesthetic concessions (Tiffin and Huggan 14). Throughout the novel, the narrator strives to comprehend why the President is so evil, but is opposed by the Author that this cannot be understood only with individualistic theories and reductionist dualities such as nature against culture (109). In the part where he learns that the Author is arrested as a fugitive political criminal, who is hinted to have suffered from the oppression perpetuated by the President during his term as the commander-in-chief, the narrator openly raises his voice against the latter for the first time: "On this island our friend represents good, and you represent evil" (169). But, as the Author has pointed out, such essentialist perspectives are insufficient to comprehend the multitudes behind this evil, that is, behind "the majority dictatorship," an expression Livaneli thinks that describes the cruel games

disguised as democracy (189).[5] Here the Author in the story coincides with
the author of *Son Ada* by discussing the questions Livaneli has posed. The
President and his followers are in fact products of the same system, incul-
cated with the fear of enemies and domestic threats. Having the courage to
question and fight against injustice and violence together could be the only
meaningful response to evil regardless of its causes, sources, or targets.

In the closing chapter of the novel, it is revealed that *Son Ada* is presented
as the memoir of the narrator who is eventually sent to prison with the
rest of the islanders. In his narrative that shifts between the first and the
second person point of view, he now regrets that unlike the Author, he fails
to oppose the President firmly from the very beginning to prevent what is
to follow: "We should have rebelled back when those trees were cut, and
the grocer's innocent son was beaten. [...] We naively accepted every step
the President has taken. The seagulls, on the other hand, won because they
resisted and refused to compromise" (181). These remorseful words are
by no means optimistic; neither is the novel itself with the catastrophes it
portrays.

However, as Søren Baggesen points out, "there isn't just one brand of
pessimism; there are pessimisms" (35). Livaneli's perspective exemplifies
"utopian pessimism" in Baggesen's terms: although he approaches evil and
violence as "an inextricable part of the human condition," he considers it
within the context of historical realities and future possibilities, not only
anti-utopian but also eutopian, rather than "a metaphysical (or ontological) necessity" that forecloses the possibility of a better course of action
(Baggesen 40). At this point, reminiscent of a familiar plot device in dystopian fiction, that is, the secretly written and eventually published narrative
in the storyline, the book itself becomes the pessimistic hope and fictional
admonition via its self-reflexive quality. The narrator writes, "If this manuscript is to be published one day, the editor will remove the redundant
paragraphs" (30). Later, he swears that he will "publish the book and present it to people" as a tribute to his friend who always "feels obliged to
tell the truth [...] and chooses to be a part of an honourable and beautiful
movement over being a saviour" (171). The book the readers physically

---

5   From the interview included in the Appendix at the end of the book.

hold in their hands indicates that the narrator has succeeded. Livaneli makes a critical /aesthetic intervention, which confronts the President's hegemonic intervention through the narrator's perseverance, and gestures towards the eutopian transformation of the material world.

Son Ada demonstrates that neither ahistorical safety havens nor "saviours" will help; but also dictators come and go in the end, albeit the difficulty of believing so. It is the grocer's voiceless son –voiceless both because of his speech impediment and of people's indifference towards him – that cannot overlook cruelty and puts an end to the President's life by sacrificing his own life too. This is an important symbolic moment insofar as it represents an act of resistance by and for the marginalized to regain their voice. Nevertheless, it is still a singular act that can only partially solve the problem notwithstanding its tragic magnitude. Livaneli reminds the readers that only responsible and collective action against oppression, that is, the power to say "no" in solidarity can alleviate, if not eradicate, the socio-political and environmental crises of history. His utopian pessimism that hopes for a more liveable world for both human and non-human residents of the earth is located in the "back then" of the narrator, which is and should always be our now if we want to break hegemonic cycles and stand against unjust authorities from the very beginning before it is too late. If "everything is connected to everything else," then survival depends not on coercion but on coexistence of beliefs, worldviews, and species.

Works Cited

Armillas-Tiseyra, Magali. *The Dictator Novel: Writers and Politics in the Global South*. Northwestern UP, 2019.

Baggesen, R. M. P., and Søren Baggesen. "Utopian and Dystopian Pessimism: Le Guin's *The Word for World Is Forest* and Tiptree's *We Who Stole the Dream*." *Science Fiction Studies*, vol. 14, no. 1, 1987, pp. 34–43. *JSTOR*, www.jstor.org/stable/4239792. Accessed 28 Apr. 2020.

Bakhtin, Mikhail M. "Forms of Time and of the Chronotope in the Novel: Notes toward a Historical Poetics." Mikhail M. Bakhtin. *The Dialogic Imagination: Four Essays*, edited by Michael Holquist.

Translated by Caryl Emerson and Michael Holquist. 1981. Austin: University of Texas Press, 1990. pp. 84–258.

Commoner, Barry. *The Closing Circle.* 1971. Dover Publications, 2020.

Deleuze, Gilles. *Desert Islands and Other Texts: 1953–1974.* Translated by Michael Taormina, Semiotext (e) Foreign Agents Series, 2004.

Gottlieb, Erika. *Dystopian Fiction East and West: Universe of Terror and Trial.* McGill-Queen's UP, 2001.

Göktürk, Akşit. *Ada: İngiliz Yazınında Ada Kavramı.* 1973. Yapı Kredi Yayınları, 1997.

Huggan, Graham and Helen Tiffin. *Postcolonial Ecocriticism: Literature, Animals, Environment.* Routledge, 2010.

Jameson, Fredric. "Third-World Literature in the Era of Multinational Capitalism." *Social Text*, vol 15, 1986, pp. 65–88.

Livaneli, Zülfü. *Son Ada.* Doğan Kitap, 2018.

Livaneli Zülfü. "Edebiyatta Diktatörler." *Demokrat Haber*, 8 April 2012, https://www.demokrathaber.org/edebiyatta-diktatorler-makale,4679.html. Accessed 28 April 2020.

Plumwood, Val. *Environmental Culture: The Ecological Crisis of Reason.* Routledge, 2001.

Ayşe Beyza Artukarslan

The Cat, the Cock, the Maid and Zeberjet: The Animals of *Motherland Hotel*

"Soiling yourself was beyond your control." (2017, p. 42)[1]
Motherland Hotel, narrating the hotel clerk Zeberjet's last days is one of the most influential novels of modern Turkish literature of the 20th century. The unfortunate tale of Zeberjet begins and ends in the hotel he works as his father did before him. The novel begins three days after a mysterious customer's – "the woman off the delayed train from Ankara" (2017, p. 9) – departure after spending a night in the hotel. The woman has such an impact on Zeberjet that on the hope of her return Zeberjet leaves the hotel next day, buys new clothes for himself and has his moustache shaved. When he gives up on that hope, he ends up killing the maid and the cat of the hotel then himself in the same room he was born in thirty-three years ago. The novel invites many-folded readings of the place, psychoanalysis and feminist studies. However, I intend to discover the animality of Zeberjet along with the other animals, both human like the maid of the hotel, and nonhuman like the black cat of the hotel and gamecocks, in the novel. Read in this way, *Motherland Hotel* introduces us to ourselves as the subject of the ecological crisis in the world. It is undeniable that the current environmental problems has only one subject, humans. Humanity is like a virus systematically killing its host at all costs, which I believe stems from the problem of subjecthood. Once the subjecthood is established, everything else becomes objects to be eaten, beaten, killed or exploited. However, the earth tells our tale with a different wording; more than the subject who built this world, we are one of many who are allowed to live. Humanity is stuck in between referring to itself as an independent ethical subject and accepting itself as part of an environment it depends

---

1   Throughout this article, quotations of *Motherland Hotel* will be from the translation made by Fred Stark, City Light Publishers, Kindle Edition.

on like other animals. To be more precise, it struggles between Kantian[2] ethical subjecthood and a symbiotic one. In that sense, Zeberjet allows us to examine this struggle in his quest to establish a male subjecthood throughout the novel.

Subjecthood is undeniably one of the most important gifts we are given by the Western thought. Many other features attributed to humans and believed to separate them from animals essentially like reason, will or language concern the ability of being a subject. This ability is discussed to a great extent in the works of Immanuel Kant who believes that even though it is human's natural right to be a subject, it is also human's duty to deserve this subjecthood. In Kantian philosophy, humans are reminded of the meaning and aim of being in this world very often. Even though Kant does not deny the animality of human, he establishes a nuanced hierarchy. According to him, "[m]an in the system of nature (homo phaenomenon, animal rationale ["Man as a phenomenon, rational animal[3]"] is a being of little significance and, along with the other animals, considered as products of the earth, has an ordinary value (pretium vulgare)" (Kant, 1964, p. 95). The only way to exceed this ordinary value and to be able to gain an extraordinary worth is through being "the subject of morally-practical reason" (p. 96). For Kant, human holds "an absolute inner worth" (p. 97) on top of Aristotle's rationale and Descartes' cogito. Still, he does not claim that there would be something left living when the human body is gone as Descartes does; Kant does not deny the material existence of the human body. Yet, the worth he attributes to human comes directly from something that is inner. Therefore, it is up to the human to regard "himself as a sensible being (according to his animal nature) or as an intelligible being (according to his moral predisposition)" through the will he holds, however "his insignificance as a human animal cannot injure the

---

2   I am aware that Immanuel Kant is neither the first nor the last of the thinkers who pondered on the *man's* subjecthood. Yet, I choose him among others because, as it will be explained, he establishes an elaborate way to protect this subjecthood, and he is one of the few who recognises man's responsibility toward the *lesser*.

3   Even though Socrates's "animal rationale" is considered as the first separation of *man* from his animality, Kant diminishes its importance here only to propose responsibility of dignity of *man*.

consciousness of his dignity as a rational man" (p. 97). Kant here names
what that absolute inner worth is; it is the dignity of being human. Even
though human should "live accordance with nature" they should also
make themselves "even more perfect than nature created" them (p. 79)
as an outcome of the responsibility of this dignity.[4] In *Motherland Hotel*
the dignity of being human and furthermore of being a male subject is
bestowed upon Zeberjet. However, it is a great burden to carry.

Zeberjet

> Of not quite average height, but not particularly short either. In the army they
> had him listed at 5'4" and 119 pounds. Now, at the age of thirty-three, he could
> strip and weigh in at 124 or 5. For the past two years his stomach muscles have
> been going flabby. Head too large for his body, high forehead. Hair, eyebrows,
> eyes and mustache are brown. A pinched face, somewhat downturned but not,
> after all, as much as he found its reflection that morning, when the woman off
> the Ankara train had left. Small hands, stubby fingernails. Narrow shoulders and
> chest. He was born at seven months. (, 2017, p. 15)

Born as a premature baby, Zeberjet's appearance troubles him throughout
his life. Even his name was given because of his size – " 'Call him
Zeberjet—peridot.' " (2017, p. 16) – and in school he was mocked – "[A]
boy had made up a rhyme to taunt him with. Muhittin used to sing, 'His
mother thought she bore a son, but Zeberjet kneads buns.' " – (p. 34).
The woman who worked in the brothel he used to visit when he was
in the army would call him "my little soldier" and pointing to his erect
penis once said: "Well look at that… It's about as big as the rest of you"
(p. 33). As Zeberjet's physicality shadows the subjecthood he would like
to establish, the narrator pays attention to other men's physical appearance, especially on their moustaches in the narrative many times. If this
moustache narrative is followed, often the men with the moustache show
a greater virility than Zeberjet – "[Zeberjet] stiffened and turned, his
heart pounding. The mustached customer had gotten up from his bench
and was standing next to him with a glare" (p. 95) – by diminishing his

---

4   In his guidelines to perfect human, Kant, suggests a set of exercises to elevate the
    spirit of human, one of which is called interestingly "true gymnastics" (p. 109)
    as if to suggest literally running from animality.

manhood. At the beginning of the novel, Zeberjet has a "trim, square mustache" (p. 26) and after seeing himself in the mirror of the room that the woman off the delayed train from Ankara spent the night, Zeberjet decides to change his looks in the hope of her return. Getting rid of his moustache is the first step. However, the barber in the town who would already symbolically castrate (Sozalan, 2014, p. 243) his manhood by shaving off his moustache, causes him even further harm when he does not recognize the hairy patch over his lips as a moustache.[5] When Zeberjet asks him to "[z]ip off the mustache, too," the barber laughs and says, "[y]ou're quite the kidder" (2017, p. 26). This castration motif continues along with people who would not recognize the fact that he got his moustache shaved, or with a hotel customer who fails to remember if he had a moustache at all before.

As Zeberjet's masculine subjecthood is an undercurrent narrative of the novel, not just the moustache, but everything he fails to attain seems to be working against him. The chain of events ending with the murder of the maid and the cat, and Zeberjet's suicide begins with the problem of identification for Zeberjet. He could not find any one like himself. His looks, his job, his name are all peculiar. He longs to belong to something common, something ordinary. That is why one night he decides to write his own name into the record book of the hotel. "In all these years not one Zeberjet had come in. He put down Zeberjet Gezgin for Room 5" (p. 48). He has never met someone like himself. Even though he inherited his father's leather wallet, his pocket watch, his job and this manor, he simply cannot fill in his father's shoes. He is unable to be like his father who had died sitting on the same chair he sits now. "Sixty-three years old, he died in his chair behind the tall half-moon desk one spring morning (p. 17)." This identity crisis shows itself when he lies about his name to the boy he meets during the cockfight. "What was his name? Ekrem. The boy asked too, and Zeberjet lit his cigarette before answering. 'Ahmet' "

---

5   In her article "The Woman who Spent the Night in Motherland Hotel," published in *Kadınlar Dile Düşünce* [*When Women Fall into the Language*] (2014), Ozden Sozalan does a feminist deconstructive reading of the novel. From here on, I translate the quotations from this article.

(p. 59). After writing down his unique name on the record book in the hope that there could be other Zeberjets in this world, this time he tries to create a new identity by christening himself with one of the most popular names in Turkey.

Zeberjet's family line is another way for him to relate to this world. We often find Zeberjet contemplating upon his heritage and the history of the manor house before it turned into a hotel. This repeated contemplation is a way for Zeberjet to assure himself about the legitimacy of his existence in the world. His whole life is based upon a heritage he could not dare leaving behind. A heritage he does not own. Zeberjet's maternal grandmother gives birth to a daughter, Zeberjet's mother, after her rape by the owner of the manor house, long before it turns into a hotel. Even his relation to the owners of the hotel, the Kecheji family, is blurred. The last Kecheji, a man who was named after one of the family members who hanged himself in the manor house at the age of nineteen, Faruk Kecheji now lives in Istanbul. He came "down from Istanbul five years ago for the sale of his two shops, had promised not to give up the hotel, laughing, 'It keeps me in cigarettes'" (p. 118). The hotel as the only thing that gives Zeberjet a reason to wake up in the morning exists for Faruk Kecheji only to buy more cigarettes. The only place for which he owns the keys is of little importance for this other heir of the family. Zeberjet's rooted dislike of him is revealed when he is about to commit suicide. "Last of the Kechejis. You couldn't count the one in Istanbul who had forgotten the house he was born in" (p. 117). Even though both Faruk Kecheji and Zeberjet were born in the same bed, in the same room of this house, only one could be the true heir of the family. Of course, it would be the one who did not leave the place and the one who would take his life in the room he was born, in the same way the other Faruk of the family did, by hanging himself from the ceiling. This suicide, I believe, is the only act Zeberjet performs to establish a real identity. By this act, he attempts to dispel the curse of being a bastard/foster son of Kechejis and really turn himself into a native son. Before "salvation" comes in the form of suicide, however, Zeberjet tries other ways to found his subjecthood on and he witnesses other men doing the same. The first victim of this search is a cock.

The Cock

Zeberjet comes across a cockfight six days after the arrival of the woman off the delayed train from Ankara, on the day he gives up on his hopes of her return – "Suppose he put on his old clothes tomorrow, started letting his mustache grow." (2017, p. 56) – and stops admitting any customers in the hotel. He follows the two men talking about cockfights to Spur and Beak Café[6] where the spectators bet on their favorite cocks. Since the regulars of this place know the possibility of this sweet profit, they are quite respectful to the animal they favor.

> The one in the corner let out a brief, hoarse crow. The other, near the door, stretched its neck to see, gave an equally brief crow, and crapped on the table. People laughed. A happy-faced, rotund man took out a handkerchief and cleaned up the droppings with all the concentration one might bestow on some precious substance. He smoothed the fowl's neck and praised him. (p. 56)

Patricia Jones gives a candid testimony on her view of gamecocks as someone who works in a rehabilitation center for ex-gamecocks.[7] She claims that before they come together with the other animal, the cocks are injected with testosterone or methamphetamine, they are kept in individual cages where it is impossible to socialize and therefore to behave in the way nature intended them to be (Jones, 2011, p. 45). As Jones underlines, there is a long tradition of this animal's association with masculinity. That is the reason why the other meaning of the word cock is the penis of male human. Moreover, that is the reason why in the novel the owner of the cock who has lost the fight performs a show of immense violence towards his animal. The owners of these gamecocks see their animals as an extension of their masculinity, and when their rooster has lost, they feel ashamed as if they have lost their own manhood. It is an end to their manhood and consequently to their subjecthood when the animal quite naturally wants to keep away from an attacker. Despite this view, as Jones explains, cocks are highly sensitive

---

6 A café where weekly-organised cockfights are held in the novel.

7 Her article "fighting cocks" was published in *Sister Species* (2011) edited by Lisa Kemmerer where women animal activists share their first-hand experiences with animals.

animals. "In contrast to the myth of male stoicism, roosters tend to be more emotional than hens, probably because they need to be more sensitive to potential threats" (p. 54). However, these animals deprived of everything in their nature as they are deprived of their freedom, beak the opponent to death, even though that is not something they would do in their natural state.

> No one set foot in the pit. The fight went on. The short-crested cock couldn't shake free. He fell attempting to leap, got up, staggered. The other bird put all he had left into a double-winged blow that finished him. He lay still, neck and body stretched full length. The owners came to pit center, where the exhausted but still standing cock was gathered up affectionately. The thick-browed losing owner grasped his yellow, red and black bird by the legs and swung it with a thud against the pit floor. Then he let fly with it over toward the arcade. The neck stretched longer as the bird arced across to fall between two of the small domes. (2017, p. 58)
>
> Seeing that his manhood is killed beak by beak by the other cock, the owner keeps his animal in the game in spite of the warnings from the audience – "It's murder." "Get him out of here. Break it up." (p. 58) – and then he kills his rooster by thudding it against the floor. This is his attempt to regain his manhood; the subjecthood he believes he has established through violence could only be redeemed by another, more violent act. During all this in Spur and Beak Café, Zeberjet seems to be frightened by this violence and he has been distracted because of a young man he wanted to kiss on the mouth, Ekrem – "Pressing his arm against the boy's, he found it hard and warm. ... The eyes were bright, long-lashed. The boy smiled. Zeberjet had a sudden urge to lean over and kiss him, but looked away and removed his arm." (p. 58). In the way he reacts to the two men's fight in the restaurant on the same day – "While the clamor of talk rose all at once around him Zeberjet sat stiffly erect, the cigarette crushed between two fingers of his left hand." (p. 54) – Zeberjet finds himself stiffened to the point that the hotel key he holds in his hand hurts his palm. The two men and the two fighting cocks cause the same paralysis for Zeberjet even though he will eventually end up being the perpetrator of even more violent acts, only to establish his manhood, much like the owner of the defeated cock.

The Maid

The maid is another one of the animals who is stripped out of her subjecthood by being deprived of a name. Like the cat, she has a name – Zeynep – but no one uses it. Her uncle who raised this orphan girl has brought her from a village to the hotel ten years ago. He married her off at seventeen but "but toward dawn of the wedding night the groom sent her back saying he wanted a virgin[8]" (2017, p. 18). Then the uncle married her off to a widower with three children, "and before three months were out he had brought her back because she slept too much" (p. 18). Then the uncle talks about the difficulties of protecting a non-virgin and "barren" girl from the assaults of other men in the village and that is the reason why he wants Zeberjet to take her as a maid. Soon enough, Zeberjet also discovers the "allure" of a woman who sleeps heavily and does not get pregnant.

> {the maid's room, rank with sweat. She sleeps a great deal, turns in early. Every morning he has to shake her awake. At night he'll come in as a rule and lie with her. To sleep undisturbed she beds with no underthings and with legs slightly apart. When he strokes her, even when he's on her, she goes on sleeping. Sometimes he'll bite a nipple and she mumbles "Ow" or "Scat." When he's through he climbs off and uses a handkerchief to wipe her dry} (p. 10)

Zeynep is a woman Zeberjet rapes almost every night for ten years, a woman about whom Zeberjet merely thinks, "[m]aybe she had noticed. The handkerchief under her pillow would be enough" (p. 37) and cannot even be certain if she knows it or not. It seems that Zeberjet has long forgotten the responsibilities of being a Kantian ethical subject, and he is not alone at that. On the surface of the novel, the identity of the man who first raped Zeynep before she was seventeen remains a mystery since the girl did not tell it after she was sent back from the first groom in spite of the fact that her uncle beat her viciously in front of his wife – " 'Well, then, little slut, who's been in at you?' 'Dunno [sic],' she says, and won't tell. I beat her and so forth. 'I dunno [sic], honest,' is all she'll say." (p. 18). The reason he could not get an answer from her, I argue, is because it was already him who raped her. That is why she is not exactly grateful to him when he leaves her in the hotel: "He went and called up the stairs. "Zeeyy-nep! I'm leaving, you ill-bred goose, aren't you going to kiss my hand?" No answer. He shook his head. "All the best, then," and left" (p. 19). Kissing the hand of an elder person is a way of showing respect in Turkish society. Even though the uncle openly demands this respect, she declines.

---

8   In its original Turkish text the word that the uncle uses can be translated exactly into "spoilt, something that had gone bad." That is what a woman who has a premarital intercourse is accepted to be.

Another textual clue is the three words she has once muttered in her sleep when Zeberjet tried to wake her up before raping her. "He closed the door and went over, undid her buttons, took a breast in each hand, firm and full. He shook her. Not stirring she spoke in her sleep. 'That you, uncle?'" (p. 20). She is familiar with the uncle's undoing her buttons, taking her breasts in his hands and shaking her. The question of "[t]hat you, uncle?" also suggests that the rape of the uncle was not once, but it was, very much like Zeberjet's, recurrent, maybe even every night. Even after ten years, she remembers the uncle's visits to her room. In this sense, the maid stands out as a human animal in the book who is exploited many times by other human animals she was entrusted. Zeberjet and the uncle see Zeynep as a "barren" field where they can practice their masculine subjectivity without the interruptions they experience in daily life stemming from their own physical incapability, and from other more virile men in society.

Zeynep seems to be the exact opposite of Zeberjet: "Chestnut hair, deep blue eyes. A long face with a turned-up nose and toothy, full-lipped mouth. Medium height, firm and smooth-fleshed – what they call being "firm as a fish." Thirty-five years old and slightly bow-legged" (p. 18). The narrator always notes the black soles of her feet when she sleeps deeply in her bed whereas Zeberjet washes his feet every night. Zeberjet wakes up early and dresses up sharply, whereas the woman famously sleeps a lot, and does not pay attention to her underpants showing while she works. "One early afternoon of the first week she'd been down on her knees swabbing the lobby floor. Zeberjet…looked up. She was leaning forward, bloomers stretched over her copious backside." (p. 19). Zeberjet lives day to day by his routines, once or twice a year he goes to a tailor, twice a year he goes to a Turkish bath, to a barber every four weeks, and to the post office once a month to send Faruk Kecheji's share of the profit. Zeynep, on the other hand, goes out for the groceries once each week, only does what she is told daily by Zeberjet and has always a certain smell in her unaired room. With her greater bulk than Zeberjet, she almost stands out like nature herself which, despite the latter's great efforts to wake her up or turn her over, goes on sleeping even when Zeberjet is at his climax. Her indifference to both the misery and joy of the human animal never stops amazing the reader throughout the narrative. However, this indifference cannot be a sign of her consent to this objectification. According to Carol

J. Adams[9] "[o]bjectification permits an oppressor to view another being as an object" (Adams, 1990, p. 73). Zeberjet's failure as a male subject in society causes him to explore the domestic sphere as his barren field where he is the shepherd of being. Once established, this system creates its own hierarchy between the subject and the object. The end of the relationship between Zeberjet and the maid comes when Zeberjet expects more from her.

> Toward morning he'd awakened from a dream in which he was coming and coming. His briefs were wet and sticky in front. He'd sat up, and with the dripping held in his hand had gone to the bathroom. Soiling yourself was beyond your control. In his dream it had been strange to lie with the maid, whom he hadn't thought of that way lately. She'd been almost the same as in real life, but she opened her eyes, embraced him, and when he chewed her nipple said, "Haa, I'm yours," or "Ahh, how I'm yours. (2017, p. 42)

Zeberjet wants her to be willing; he wants her to desire this as much as he does. However, the maid is as indifferent as the cock whose feathers have been stroked by men while standing up right on the table and crapping on it. This indifference seems to be what brings her doom in the novel but what actually does so is a natural outcome of being an absent referent as Adams terms it. "The consumption of the referent reiterates its annihilation as a subject of importance in itself" (Adams, 1990, p. 73). Even though Adams establishes this term through the practice of meat-eating, rape also produces absent referents. In the novel, the maid only exists through the use value Zeberjet makes up for her. This is the only way he relates to her. At this point, she is not different from an animal slaughtered for its meat. Consequently, when he does not get the satisfaction he desires from her, when one night he wakes her up to see if she wants it, too, and finds her awake but unwilling, Zeberjet turns the maid into the ultimate absent referent. The woman in this way turns to be a dead body.

> He got to his knees and saw that she had her eyes shut. With a lunge he seized her throat. As she jerked violently and opened her eyes, he closed his. Her knee rammed his crotch and he clenched in pain. Something moved in the hardness under his thumbs. He heard a gurgle. Her body lashing, she clung to his wrists and he bore down with all he had, face locked, fingers locked, a roaring in his

---

9   Carol J. Adams introduces feminist vegetarian theory in her book *Sexual Politics of Meat* (1990).

ears, and the hands went limp around his wrists and all struggling ceased. He loosened his grip and slid down off the bed, only then looking. Her eyes and mouth were open. (2017, p. 69)

When Zeberjet manages to wake her during the rape she refuses to be treated like a piece of meat. When he orders her to take her shift off, she opposes him. Unaware what has been done to her for all this time, now she is awake and conscious, she struggles to cover her breasts and to stop Zeberjet. Even though it seems like the reason why Zeberjet gets furious and kills the woman, something happens in between Zeynep's gaining consciousness and her murder. "He had an erection, but when he pushed, it softened and refused to go in. He waited a moment, heart pounding, and tested it. Taking his hand away and pushing he felt it go soft, shrink" (p. 69). The maid's unwillingness causes Zeberjet to lose his erection, his failed subjecthood as a virile man.

Masterfully underlines the anonymity of Zeynep's death through one other murder we only get to know about through a courtroom hearing towards the end of the novel. In his absent-minded strolling, Zeberjet finds himself in a courtroom where a groom is being charged with the murder of his wife on their wedding night. Even though they found the body of the bride naked on the bed with "her head smashed and bloody her hair spread on the pillow" (p. 85), the doctor of the court testifies she is a virgin. The groom is called Ahmet Kuruja. Coincidentally, the name Zeberjet christened himself earlier turns out to be the name of a man who murders his wife probably from the same reason why Zeberjet killed the maid. The parallelism of the names and the parallelism in the way of both murders are committed, seem to suggest that Ahmet Kuruja has lost his erection in the way Zeberjet lost his, right when he was at the summit of his virility. This also explains why he is unwilling to reveal the reason for the murder. Ahmet stays silent but Zeberjet imagines himself answering the questions the judge asks Ahmet, as if they were concerning his murder of the maid.

'The doctor testifies she was a virgin. Her father insists he never let a male, not even a male fly near her. What made you do it?'
'Father? Her father's been long dead when they married her off the groom demanded a virgin naked that early dawn with eyes and mouth open I drew the quilt ... ' 'Tell us, now, or it will go hard with you. Speak out! Why did you kill her?' (p. 88)

This is a moment of the narrative circling around Zeberjet's thoughts that escape him. Even then, we run into other narratives like that of the cock and the nameless bride both of whom had been smashed to death. All three bodies that have been absent referents in different ways (rooster as a cockfight, the dead woman as a nameless bride and the maid as a barren field for Zeberjet to play with), become literal pieces of meat irrecoverably.

Zeynep does not remain the only one who is victimized by Zeberjet's trial to gain an absolute control over his subjects. The cat's doom will be the same.

The Cat

> Male, black. The second cat since Zeberjet took over. A tall girl in town with her father to see the ancient ruins, who stayed two nights and always carried a few horse-chestnuts in her purse, had christened the cat Lampblack. But nobody uses this name (2017, p. 20).

They have this cat because after the first one's death, the maid has said "What's a hotel without a cat?" (p. 71). There are many moments in the narrative Zeberjet seems almost haunted by this cat. He often feels the gaze of a pair of eyes on him, and when he turns back, he always finds the cat there. Whenever Zeberjet is up to no good, the cat is present. Like the time when he is in the room of the woman off the delayed train from Ankara, thinking of her, using her hand towel she forgot in the room to wipe himself after satisfying himself, the cat is there. Like when he is watching a couple having sex through the keyhole, the cat is there. A pair of eyes is always shining in the dark, always on Zeberjet. Right after the death of the maid, the cat is there again.

> A noise came and he leapt out of bed, intent, unbreathing. Upstairs. He ran up barefoot, slowing on the final flight. The cat was scratching at the door of her room. Seeing him it mewed. It liked having her near, and always spent the day around her, but had never begged this way at night when left in the hall. Sometimes when he was on her a sound under the bed, a furious scratching at the linoleum, had startled him, and he had shut the cat out of the room. He turned on the hall light and the animal mewed. What was he going to do with it? (p. 70)

This cat is reminiscent of Derrida's cat who catches the philosopher naked from time to time. When he is caught naked to his cat, he notices the way philosophers before him have always imagined a blind animal who can be seen but cannot look back. Now that he sees this animal who returns his gaze he concludes:

> The animal is there before me, there next to me, there in front of me – I who am (following) after it. And also, therefore, since it is before me, it is behind me. It surrounds me. And from the vantage of the being-there-before-me it can allow itself to be looked at, no doubt, but also – something that philosophy perhaps forgets, perhaps being this calculated forgetting itself – it can look at me. It has this point of view regarding me. The point of view of the absolute other, and nothing will have ever given me more food for thinking through this absolute al- terity of the neighbor or of the next(-door) than these moments when I see myself seen naked under gaze of a cat. (Derrida, 2008, p. 10)

The point where Derrida problematizes animal as the subject of an eth- ical discussion is when he comes up with a word: l'animot. L'animot is a hybrid word, formed by the words l'animal and mot which means the animal and word in French. He believes that the western philosophers, by using "the animal," not giving attention to the sex, to the species, to what that animal actually is, have created themselves a singular animal they place for everything that does not stand for humanity. L'animot represents the animality of animal and it makes every action towards animals legit- imate to underline the infinite alterity of animal because "[i]t is a matter of putting the animal outside of the ethical circuit" (p. 106). As once it is established, the animal lacks the inner dignity and therefore the inherent quality like in Kantian philosophy, the oldest cultural fraternal mottos of the western society, like "Love thy neighbour" or "Thou shalt not kill" are not potent for the animal object or the phrase "Know thyself" now never refers to the animality of the human. Under the gaze of his cat, Derrida questions the whole Kantian philosophy concerning the animal's stance and finds himself surrounded by the animal who can look at him when he is naked. Nakedness becomes an important issue here for Derrida because he underlines that the animal can never be naked since it does not know of it. Therefore, it is only the human who can actually be naked. Derrida finds "[n]udity is nothing other than that passivity, the involuntary exhibi- tion of the self" (p. 11). If the animal can never be naked, this involuntary exhibition of the self is only valid for the human. In the novel, Zeberjet strips the maid many times, exposing her to this involuntary passivity, and when he wishes her to voluntarily get naked, she lets him down. However, this time Zeberjet himself feels naked in the gaze of the black cat. Even though he is not naked here, Zeberjet does something to be ashamed of far greater than being naked. As it is his role to watch Zeberjet throughout the novel, it is again the cat that witnesses the death of the maid.

> Something warm and soft brushed against his leg and his head snapped up. The cat. He stroked it, full length from head to tail. The cat, purring and arching its back as he stroked, put its front paws on his leg, digging and releasing with the claws. He could feel the living warmth under his hand. He was getting a hard-on. (2017, p. 69)

Unlike the maid, the cat responds to his strokes. Later on, however, because of the fate it will share with the other animals of the novel, it does not let it go. The cat scratches the maid's door room, as if he felt the lifeless body lying in her bed. The more it wants to go into room, the more Zeberjet gets frightened of it and realizes that the only solution is to get rid of the cat. However, from this moment on, the cat begins to get aggressive. When the cat scratches his face, Zeberjet cannot help but feel amazed at how the calm creature has gotten this wild. The resistance he has not received from the maid, he receives from the cat. Of these two animals, the one that has never been transformed into an absent referent by being stripped of his clothes or being raped has a much stronger will. Still its end is not different than that the woman.

> 'Here puss, here. No one will hurt you,' and held out his left hand as though offering a scrap. The cat straightened and came slowly out. It rubbed against his hand. Animals forget so easily. He gripped the handle tight, stroking the cat with his free hand and pushing its head away. He raised the pan, snatched his hand off the cat's neck and struck, immediately jumping to his feet. The cat lay convulsing. Again, he struck it on the head. Tail and legs stiffened, there was a rigid trembling, and stillness. One eye stood out of its socket, and blood lay on the linoleum. (p. 71)

Then he throws Lampblack through the window. The cat whose name has long been forgotten becomes an absent referent and falls on the pavement across from the hotel. Like all the animals that have been and will be killed in the hands of human. "Soiling himself was beyond his control". After all Kant's ethics advises that "Towards bruta we have no immediate duty... physical instinct might well prevail, to destroy one another for the satisfaction of their needs. Yet it cannot be denied that a hard-heartedness towards animals is not in accordance with the law of reason..." (Kant, 1997, p. 435).

At being given the responsibility of the hotel – "Here in the twelve-room manor house. All yours" (2017, p. 73), Zeberjet feels like Adam in Paradise. He feels he is the shepherd of all being; all the guests that have stayed at the hotel and the people who had once inhabited the manor. Their many stories, of life and death and of every human state; the lesbian relationship of two servant women, the suicide of one of the youngest of Kechejis, the rape of a young servant girl (Zeberjet's grandmother) by the oldest of the family. Also the new stories of the hotel with each customer, stories of complete strangers to Kechejis; married couples, unmarried couples, prostitutes and their johns, two men wanting one bed, a man hiding from the police after smothering his own daughter. Motherland Hotel contains this all. Sozalan pays attention to the words "motherland" and "hotel" and believes that the discrepancy between these words – "motherland that suggests rootedness and hotel that suggests a transience" (Sozalan, 2014, p. 236). This discrepancy is not valid for the cat, the maid and Zeberjet. Everyone and everything else is transient except these three. However, as the man who holds the key, Zeberjet oversees these animals. In the traditional codes of male subjecthood, he feels they are his responsibility. However, the novel is full of *lesser*s trusted to men and they all end up being brutally murdered. This shows the problematic nature of subjecthood; when one is trusted to the other, it is stripped down of its subjecthood and becomes somewhat an object. Moreover, once something becomes an object, it becomes open to all exploitation by the subject. Zeberjet like other men in the novel exploits animals, both human and non-human, around him to the point where there is nothing left to be exploited except for his own animality. The only thing he carries is his own animal body. Still, that freedom is too heavy to a burden.

> He was still here, everything was still in his control. He could slip the rope off, wait some more, run for it, give himself up, burn down the manor house. The freedom of choice was unbearable. He knocked the table over with a push of his feet; and falling through emptiness stopped short. Eyes and mouth open, legs stiffening and threshing, he reached up in an effort to grab the rope. (What came over him? Had he thought of something left undone? Or was it the parting realization that the gift of life is unparalleled and the one task on earth is to guard it, to hold out no matter what, to stay? Or was it the flesh in mute, mindless rejection fending off death? His head was sinking. His arms dangled. A thickish ivory fluid oozed from under his shorts and down the left leg. Catching in the hairs

above his knee, it ran onto the quilt and spread. Above him the swinging rope made a creaking noise where it rubbed against the wood. (2017. pp. 127–128)

Zeberjet is the parody of a species whose members believe the only real value is the one they have been gifted with. A parody of the masculine subjecthood, even when it is not supported by the traditional values of physical appearance and social status, glorified by a humanism tainted by the endless violence it is capable of imposing on others. A parody of a manhood that is afraid of its own capability and ends itself in the same violence. A tale of a man who is soiled beyond his control.

Works Cited

Adams, Carol J. (1990). *Sexual Politics of Meat: A Feminist-Vegetarian Critical Theory*. New York: The Continuum International Publishing Group.

Atilgan, Yusuf. (2017). Motherland *Hotel*. (Stark, Fred, Trans.). San Francisco: City Light Publishers. Kindle edition.

Derrida, Jacques. (2008). *The Animal that Therefore I am*. (M.-L. Mallet, Ed., & D. Wills, Trans.) New York: Fordham University Press.

Jones, Patricia. (2011). "fighting cocks." *Sister Species: Women, Animals and Social Justice*. edited by Lisa A. Kemmerer. University of Illinois Press.

Kant, Immanuel. (1964). *The Metaphysical Principles of Virtue*. (J. Ellington, Trans.) Indianapolis: The Bobbs-Merill Company.

Kant, Immanuel. (1997). *Lectures on Ethics*. (P. Heath, Trans.). Cambridge: Cambridge University Press.

Sozalan, Ozden. (2014). "Anayurt Oteli'nde Geceleyen Kadin." *Kadinlar Dile Dusunce*, edited by Sibel Irzik and Jale Parla. Istanbul: Iletisim Yayinlari.

Zeynep Talay Turner

Grizzly Man: From the Ethics of Film to the Ethics of the Animal-Other

If we could talk to the animals, learn their languages
Think of all the things we could discuss
If we could walk with the animals, talk with the animals,
Grunt and squeak and squawk with the animals,
And they could squeak and squawk and speak and talk to us.

Doctor Dolittle, Talk to the Animals

Introduction

Grizzly Man (2005) is a documentary film by German director Werner Herzog which tells us how the amateur environmentalist-activist Timothy Treadwell spent a considerable amount of time–13 summers–with grizzly bears in Alaska before, in 2003, he and his girlfriend were eaten by one. The film mostly consists of footage from films that Treadwell himself shot, showing his interactions with grizzlies and how he, alone, almost as a warrior, fought to protect them. This footage is accompanied by interviews with friends, parents, officials, and a pilot who would take Treadwell to the "expedition" site. The documentary is of interest not only for the representation of the devoted idealist Treadwell, but also for the questions raised about the human and its relation to the animal-other.

The Question of Identity

In his short essay "Identity" the German philosopher Hans Blumenberg tells us that in the 1930s the English archaeologist Max Mallowan, the husband of Agatha Christie, was on an excavation in Mesopotamia. In his team there was an Irishman called Gallagher who had a supply of fantastic tales. Mallowan told his wife about this Irishman and in her memoirs she wrote: "He was one of those people to whom the most incredible things happen" (Blumenberg 87). One of the stories from this supply was about Gallagher's uncle who had been eaten by a crocodile in Burma. The crocodile was caught and killed; however, no one knew exactly what to do with it. In the end, Gallagher had the crocodile stuffed and sent to his aunt.

Blumenberg suggests here that "The line between piety and brutality can be very fine. The questions which the nephew gave his aunt the occasion to ask, can only be a matter of clumsy speculation" (87). One question, he suggests is this: "Did she have the murderer or the victim in the house?" (87). The answer would depend on exactly when they stuffed the animal, that is to say, on whether the victim was totally digested. But then another question arises: "Would it still have been permitted to shoot the crocodile, if too much time had already passed?" (88).

The widow was placed in an impossible situation, and we as readers may speculate about how she must have behaved. We may identify with the aunt, with the uncle, or even with the crocodile.

The irony of this story is similar to the one in *Grizzly Man*. The film starts with footage from one of Timothy Treadwell's films: Treadwell is standing in front of his camera while two grizzlies are walking about in the background. "I am a kind warrior out here," he says: "I am like a fly on the wall [. . .] Occasionally I am a challenge," but then he has to be a samurai. He is quite aware of the fact that what he is doing out there is dangerous, however, his love for these animals is such that he "will die for them," though he adds, "I will not die at their claws and paws." Immediately after this, we hear the voice of Herzog "As if there was a desire in him to leave the confinements of his humanness and bond with the bears" but "in doing so, he crossed an invisible borderline."

Around the 8th minute we encounter the first interviewee, described as an actor and a close friend. He tells us how he heard of Treadwell's death: he hears his wife screaming in the other room, he thinks that "she fell or something," then goes to the room and sees the news on television. This description without content induces in us a desire to find out exactly how he died. Fortunately, without much delay, Herzog introduces us to a second interviewee who will tell us how it happened: Willy Fulton was the pilot who flew in on the day of their death to pick Treadwell and his girlfriend Amie up. Fulton didn't see them, and he could not make his voice heard either. Then, after having seen a "nasty looking" bear coming out of the bushes, he decided to get in the plane to have a look: "Just looked down and saw a human rib cage [. . .] He was just eating that." Then they came and shot the bear: "They found Tim in" says the pilot to the accompaniment of a photograph of the bear cut open. The third interviewee Sam

Egli (Egli Air Haul) says similar things: "The bear was all cut open. It was full of people [. . .] We hauled away four garbage bags of people out of that bear."

Thus, we are gradually prepared for the event, for how Timothy the warrior, the devoted amateur environmentalist became the murderer of a bear. At this point, a Native American, Sven Haakanson, the curator of the Kodiak museum, expressed what many viewers may already have been feeling: "He tried to be a bear. He tries to act like a bear and for us on the island, you don't do that [. . .] Treadwell crossed a boundary that we have lived with for 7000 years."

Ellen Brinks claims that Treadwell's own narration, in which "he positions himself as a boy-child," (Brinks 305) is a feral tale, only in reverse. If the transition from the human-animal bond to a human-human one articulates the socially normative temporality of the feral tale, Treadwell's narration/footage takes him from "being a man to becoming a man-child, and at times, to a child attempting to divest itself of humanness altogether to become a bear" (307). However, Herzog's film can also be regarded as a feral tale, and addressing the adult rather than the child, reminds us the impassable border between humanness and animality, between civilization and wilderness. In this paper I suggest that these two opposite positions and/or the tension between them not only structures Herzog's documentary but also strengthens his own_views through the caricaturized representation of Treadwell. However, it also gives us the occasion to ask vital questions about the ethics of the director, and about the ontological status of human subjectivity.

The Ethics of the Director

The debate over the opposition between nature and culture is a familiar one. We are no longer so confident about the Enlightenment idea that nature is something which we can master. Nor is it easy simply to suggest that we go back to nature. Today, in the era of global warming and at a time when the boundaries between nature and culture became more blurred and obscure, we tend to discuss the ways in which we can have a more ethical engagement with the animal-other. One of the difficulties in establishing a symmetrical relationship between animals and humans is our concepts of subjectivity, conscious thought and language which are the basis for seeing ourselves as ethical agents. In *Being and Time,* Heidegger claims that we "dwell in language," while anxiety is the primordial state of mind which is shared only by human beings (Heidegger 228–235); Kantian ethics, so influential, is based on reason, autonomy, free will which animals are held not to possess; by contrast, Spinoza claims that the difference between the human mind and the animal mind is a matter of degree, and that the lower animals also feel things, however, he also states that since we need to pursue our own advantage in life, we can treat animals in terms of their convenience for us (Spinoza 102, 134).[1] Even Nietzsche who otherwise argues that culture by suppressing our animality wishes to tame the human-animal, claims that animals are *ahistorical* beings and as such do not have a sense of temporality–a relationship between their past, present and future, beyond searching for food or shelter (Nietzsche 60–61).[2]

It might be true that unlike human beings, animals are not rational, that they cannot think, or at least not as human beings, that they do not "dwell in language," and that these differences might establish an ontological difference between animals and human beings. However, this difference becomes problematic when and/or if it also gives way to a hierarchical structure in which human beings inhabit/occupy a superior position. After all, isn't it we, human beings, who "invent" concepts (rationality, ontology, hierarchy etc.) and "name" things and while naming dominate them?[3]

---

1   On Spinoza and animal ethics see Margaret Wilson, 336–352; and as a response see John Grey, 367–388.

2   In the second essay of *On the Genealogy of Morality*, Nietzsche says that human beings are capable of promising. To promise in German is *versprechen*, which is derived from *sprechen*, that is to speak (Nietzsche 35).

3   In a different context Blumenberg draws our attention to the biblical story of the beginning and giving names in Paradise (Blumenberg, *Work on Myth*, 35): In the beginning the earth was formless and void but God said "Let there be light; and there was light." By naming things God created them. But the idea that "all trust in the world begins with names" is characteristic of science too: "the faith that the suitable naming of things will suspend the enmity between them and man, turning it into a relationship of pure serviceability. The fright that has found the way back to language has already been endured" (Blumenberg 35).

In his "The Historical Roots of Our Ecological Crisis" Lynn White investigates the theological background to such a hierarchical structure: while the idea of beginning was impossible in the Greco-Roman cyclical notion of time, Christianity inherited from Judaism, on the one hand, a new conception of time, that is as nonrepetitive and linear, on the other hand, a striking story of creation: "By gradual stages God had created light and darkness, the heavenly bodies, the earth and all its plants, animals, birds and fishes" (White 1205). Finally, God had created Adam and also as an afterthought Eve, so that Adam would not feel lonely. Man, naming all animals, established his dominance over them: "God planned all of this explicitly for man's benefit and rule: no item in the physical creation had any purpose save to serve man's purposes. And, although man's body is made of clay, he is not simply part of nature: he is made in God's image" (1205).[4] Derrida reminds us another consequence of this: "It is generally thought [. . .] what in the last instance distinguishes them [animals] from man, is their being naked without knowing it. Not being naked therefore, not having knowledge of their nudity, in short, without consciousness of good and evil" (Derrida 4–5).

In *A Thousand Plateaus,* Deleuze and Guattari attempt to overcome the hierarchical structure that human beings imposed on themselves by introducing the idea of "becoming-animal" which requires the dissolution of the subjectivities, even the humanness of humans, and of the boundaries between human and human, human and the animal, and even between the human and inanimate beings (we will come to that).[5] Is this what Treadwell was attempting?

---

4   In fact, Christianity alone is not to blame for this hierarchical structure. After all, we already had such structure in the Greco-Roman culture. For instance, Aristotle in his *History of Animals* claims that since animals lack reason, there cannot be a kinship between animals and human beings. His conceptualisation of species in which human beings are at the top, insects at the bottom, later, in medieval Christianity, came to be known as the "Great Chain of Beings" where God is at the top, Angelic beings are below God, humans are below Angelic beings and animals are below human beings. On this see Arthur O. Lovejoy, *The Great Chain of Beings: A Study of the History of an Idea.*

5   Fortunately we did not have to wait until the 20th Century to hear about being ethical towards animals: Montaigne in his "An Apology for Raymond Sebond" questioned the so-called superiority of humans over animals and argued that just like human beings, animals also deserve justice; or Bentham

According to Herzog, Treadwell, almost in a spiritualistic or religious way sought unity with nature. We are told about this desire for disremembering his identity by almost every interviewee: Larry von Daele (the bear biologist): "He would act like a bear [. . .] because it is a simpler world;" Marnie Gaede (friend/ecologist): "He wanted to become like the bear;" Sam Egli (Egli Air Haul): "But to me he was acting like he was working with people wearing bear costumes out there [. . .];" Sven Haakanson (the curator of Kodiak museum): "He tried to act like a bear." However, we are constantly reminded of the fact that in the end Treadwell cannot forget his language; he "dwells in language."

Herzog sees Treadwell as a sentimentalist or a "spiritual idealist" who devoted himself to the protection of animals. Herzog's position, however, is clear: "he agrees with Treadwell" about the foundational distinction between nature and humanity; he is fascinated by the indifference of nature, accordingly, by the aspirations but also the limits of the human. As Jeong and Andrew put it: "Herzog made his reputation in the savage outdoors, straining against every limit by which civilization defines what a human being is" (Jeong and Andrew 2). However, he repeatedly warns us against the attempt to go beyond the invisible borderline. The film starts and ends with Herzog's rather explicit statements about his own view about nature. As we have seen, at the very beginning he says: "As if there was a desire in him to leave the confinements of his humanness and bond with the bears" but "in doing so, he crossed an invisible borderline." Towards the end: "I believe that the common denominator of the universe is not harmony but chaos, hostility and murder [. . .] I see only the overwhelming indifference of nature."

On the one hand, he seems to respect Treadwell not only by making him the subject of his documentary but also by taking him seriously as a rational human being with whom he establishes a dialogue ("I disagree

---

in his *Principles of Morals and Legislation* argues that since animals, just like human beings, can also suffer, the ethical and moral questions concerning human beings need be extended to them too. Peter Singer, one of the most influential living philosophers, adopts a utilitarian approach towards animals, claiming that animals also have rights. See Peter Singer, "Animal Liberation or Animal Rights?" 3–14; also see his "All Animals are Equal," 215–229.

with Treadwell about this"); on the other hand, he represents him as an idiotic child who had some problems in the world of humans, who, as a result, claimed a place in the world of animals. How can Herzog maintain this representation of Treadwell? Simply, by means of his particular narration, as we shall see.

Though during the first half Herzog draws our attention to Treadwell's desire to dissolve his identity and to become like an animal, around half-way through the film some other features of Treadwell, other than his being an amateur, enthusiastic environmentalist, are presented. For instance, Treadwell the highly methodical filmmaker appears, repeating the same scene fifteen times. Then, we see Treadwell trying to hide himself from some enemies: "I must hide from authorities, from people who would harm me, from people who would seek me out as a story [. . .] I must be a spirit in the wilderness." Just after this, we find out that, in fact, Treadwell had had some difficulties with women and that he was drinking a lot. Further footage of Treadwell follows: he and Amie are unloading their kit from the plane, but Treadwell does not want Amie to be in shot because: "I am supposed to be alone here." Then, we hear Herzog again: "Part of the mythical character Treadwell was transforming himself into required him to be seen as being completely alone." Amie appears twice in over 100 hours of video. However, Herzog insists that we never see Amie's face properly and that she remains a mystery, even though her face is visible. Strangely enough, Herzog's voice which is ever present and gives him a "God's eye view," makes us almost believe what he says, even though our eyes tell us the opposite. As Eric Ames says, Herzog's vocal presence "not only helps establish the identity and difference of self and other but also positions Herzog as the film's source of narrative authority. He provides the controlling perspective" (Ames 246).

Then there is an interview with Treadwell's parents, in a room full of Teddy bears. After saying "Teddy bears meant a lot to him," Herzog lets the parents talk about their son: "He really wanted a new start. A fresh start [. . .] He went to California [. . .] He did change his name because it was theatrical," says the mother. The father adds that Treadwell, in fact, was encouraged to get a job on a television show, and yet, things did not work out which, according to the father, affected him deeply. Just after this, we hear the friend saying: "He had this Prince Valiant haircut. He could surf and go under water and yet still that hair would hide his receding hairline." Suddenly we see Treadwell, in front of his camera saying, "How does the hair look?" Then the friend again: "He invented a new Persona." And Herzog again: "Treadwell's need to invent a new persona for himself led him to elaborate fabrications. He claimed to be an orphan from Australia [. . .]" We hear all about this before his friend Jewel to whom a kind of authority has been given (she keeps the recording and some other belongings of Treadwell) tells us how, at some point, Treadwell was given some antidepressants, but after a while stopped taking them.

The sequence of Herzog's narration is rather explicitly leading us towards the conclusion that Treadwell was not only a sentimentalist or a "spiritual idealist" who devoted himself to the protection of animals, but more importantly a psychologically troubled man, or a man-child who suffered the brutality of the world of humanity and longed for a remedy in the world of animals. Our seeing Treadwell in his tent lying next to his Teddy bear, after pleading with God or a higher power (another with whom dialogue is impossible) to bring rain is not a coincidence. Nor, soon after this scene, is our seeing the biologist again telling us that in fact there is a stable bear population and that the biologists there are doing what should be done for the sustainability of their habitat. Herzog wants us to believe that Treadwell adopted an illusionary vision of his life, created some enemies (hunters and poachers) who did not exist and in order to do so first had to invent a new persona. But why would he do that? According to Herzog, "Timothy Treadwell, the avowed bear man of the Alaska wilderness, lived poor and little known for most of his 46 years despite a desire for the spotlight of celebrity."[6]

Herzog's position is strengthened further by the following scene, which, I think, is the key moment in the film. Just after we find out that there is actually a recording of Amie's and Treadwell's last moments, we are encouraged to want to hear this. However, this privilege is only given to Herzog whom we see (for the first and only time) listening to the

---

6   The Official web-site of Werner Herzog: http://www.wernerherzog.com/films. html. I contacted the people who prepared the web-site to find out whether Herzog himself wrote the summaries of the films on the web-site. I was informed that he did not, though that does not mean that he did not endorse them.

recording. We don't see his face completely, only the side of it from the back, and he reports what he hears to Jewel, the friend who now keeps the recording (though she herself has not listened to it): "Treadwell is saying 'Run away, Amie.'" Then, he wants Jewel to turn the recording off, before he says: "Jewel, you must never listen to this [. . .] And you must never look at the photos that I have seen at the coroner's office." Despite our knowing that we will never be allowed to listen to these recordings, nor to see the photographs till the end of the film, we will not give up the idea that we might be so allowed. This lack fosters our desire to hear their last words. Put another way, the more Herzog's "controlling perspective" and didactic position are strengthened, the more we are in his hands. As Ames writes: "Apart from any practical reasons concerning access to material, the entire scene works to distinguish Herzog, as a filmmaker who confronts death, from others, who should avert their eyes and ostensibly need to be protected" (Ames 253). Now, Herzog is the feral tale narrator who warns us against the dangers of transgressing the invisible border, that is, culture and nature, or life and death, and who, in doing so, maintains the human/animal divide.

In fact, from the beginning, the presence of Treadwell's death–even though visually it is absent–accompanies every word. The coroner's verbal account of the moment of death based on his examination of the audio-tape and of what is left of Treadwell and Amie, is a vital move: "Visual and narrative excess thus compensate for the absence of sight and sound, transforming an ethical moment into an opportunity for dramatic storytelling. The moment of death here is not just retold. It is reenacted." (Ames 253).

In *Poetry, Language, Thought* Heidegger writes: "[. . .] mortals are [. . .] human beings. They are called mortals because they can die. To die means to be capable of death as death. Only man dies, and indeed continually, as long as he remains on earth, under the sky, before the divinities" (Heidegger 150). As Silverman says: "We are headed from the first breath we take toward a death that is both 'certain' and 'indefinite,' and neither the limits of our being nor the limits of our knowledge can be 'outstripped'" (Silverman 327). However, recalling that it is in throwness where *Dasein* understands itself in its possibilities, Being-toward-death, "should not be confused with the termination of the existence; it is more a way of inhabiting the world than of leaving it" (326). Thanks to this capability of "inhabiting the world," Heidegger says, the human being is "world-forming" (Heidegger, *The Fundamental Concepts of Metaphysics*, 177). Animals, on the other hand, are considered as *animate* (that which lives, even undying) and they are "poor in world" (177). They cannot express their feelings about death, about their own death. They can scream when hunted and when preyed upon by other animals.

> Herzog seems to agree with this:
> What haunts me is that in all the faces of all the bears that Treadwell ever filmed, I discovered no kinship, no understanding, no mercy. I see only the overwhelming indifference of nature. To me there is no such thing as a secret world of bears. And this blank stare speaks only of a half-bored interest in food. But for Timothy Treadwell, this bear was a friend, a saviour.

Herzog says this over footage that was shot shortly before the bear confirmed Herzog's view of it by eating Treadwell rather than seeing him as a friend. And, in fact, this is the culmination of the narrative that Herzog has been preparing us for. Treadwell's death has already been anticipated and objectified from the beginning. Recall the first few interviewees: the pilot: "They found Tim in"; Sam Egli: "The bear was all cut open. It was full of people [. . .] we hauled away four garbage bags of people out of that bear [. . .]" And later on we hear the investigator who is showing us the metal can in which Treadwell and Amie were carried: "In the case of Treadwell and Amie, what I had were body parts." In the end, he dies like an animal: preyed upon by another animal, "moaning" during his last moments.

What kind of reaction does Herzog want us to give to Treadwell's death? Are we supposed to be disturbed by his dying like an animal? Or, precisely because Treadwell thought that he could cross the boundary between the human and the animal, in other words, he could not be "rational" and accordingly "human" enough, are we supposed to think that he deserved this death?

Becoming-Animal

It might be true that animals do not "dwell in language" but that need not mean that they do not speak. The language of the animal is, Derrida says, the language of the mute, and we need to try to hear and listen to it, for this language, or any language other than "our own," is the language of the other, of difference. In its muteness "Nature (and animality within it) is sad" says Derrida, but not because it is mute, rather "it is nature's sadness or mourning that renders it mute and aphasic, that leaves it without words" (Derrida 19). To listen to and/or hear the language of the animal is to give up those habits of thought that prepare the ground for the idea of the domination of nature.

In *Adam and Eve*, Lucas Cranach the Elder depicts animals who would not normally sit next to each other in peace in nature: a lion is lying down next to a deer who is standing next to birds and, they all – including the snake – are beside Adam and Eve. This is the depiction of the Garden of Eden at the moment just before Adam has been tempted by Eve's offer to eat the Fruit, just before the original sin. Animals are side by side indifferently because the history of humanity has not begun yet, and as such, their nature has not been determined. Agamben refers to a similar depiction from a Hebrew Bible from the 13th century, but this time it is not the depiction of the beginning but the end of the history of humanity: the miniature that interests Agamben in the Hebrew Bible represents the messianic banquet of the righteous on the last day. What is surprising to Agamben is that the righteous were represented not with human faces but with animal heads. He says that scholars who have occupied themselves with the question of why this would be so have not come up with a convincing explanation. One answer, he says, might come from the messianic prophecy of Isaiah 11:6, where the idea that animal nature will be transfigured in the messianic kingdom is implied: "the wolf shall live with the sheep,/and the leopard lie down with the kid;/the calf and the young lion shall grow up together,/and a little child shall lead them." Agamben says: "It is not impossible, therefore [. . .] the artist of the manuscript in the Ambrosian intended to suggest that on the last day, the relations between animals and men will take on a new form, and that man himself will be reconciled with his animal nature" (Agamben 3). This idea, however, is far from comforting, for the question remains: is the border between humanness and animality impassable as long as we are within the history (that begins in the Garden of Eden)?

Deleuze's and Guattari's "becoming-animal" seems to apply that it is passable, that the border can be crossed. However, "becoming-animal" does not literally mean becoming an animal; rather it is giving up the idea of a core identity and of human essence, and instead welcoming the idea of becoming, which, primarily, involves the idea of becoming other than one's own "self" with every new encounter, whether this encounter be an idea or a person or an animal or an object. This primary welcoming can also be regarded as a precondition for welcoming the other in his/her/its otherness: "We can be thrown into a becoming by anything at all, by the most unexpected, most insignificant of things. You do not deviate from the majority unless there is a little detail that starts to swell and carries you off" (Deleuze and Guattari 292). It is going beyond dualisms (man/ woman, culture/nature, black/white, chaos/cosmos etc.) and replacing them with connections, interconnections, transformations and flows: it is "to experience interchange" and "to question the ideals of humanism and purity" (Birke and Parisi 67) or indeed proposing an anti-humanism.

Positioning himself as a man-child, Treadwell refuses "to adopt the mature masculinity of the hunter/scientist that demands men keep wild animals at a distance (in order to enable the killing of, or rational control over, animals)" (Brinks 306), however, there is more to it: he seeks physical contact with the animals, he speaks to them, or rather *growls* and *snarls* with them, and in doing so he longs for "going feral" (312), for becoming-animal. It is a process of the dissolution of the subject. As Brinks argues "Treadwell's mimesis enables him to become, or to put himself in the place of the animal other, while experiencing the animal as equivalent, yet different" (315). Here Brinks uses the term mimesis in a specific way: it is not simply an imitation of nature or a matter of representation; rather it is a process of "unselfing" (314). How? It primarily relies on voice and proprioception, "that inner sense of where the different parts of one's own body are in relation to one another," or in other words, a sensory modality which enables "thinking through body" (313). This idea of "thinking through body" is compatible with the idea of becoming-animal, which is not about what a body or a subjectivity is, but rather what a body, a plane of affects, is capable of. For instance, in fearful situations we experience physiological changes: such as increased heart rate, sweating etc. We may even go through some hormonal, musculoskeletal and neural changes, however remain unconscious. Such a state, as Steve Baker argues, "opens the body to intensity and [unmakes] the secure and fearful self" (Quoted in Brinks 313). If this kind of corporeal understanding is performative by nature, it may then provide us with a new approach to the conceptualisation of the self and other relationship, and what we see in Treadwell's mimetic performance is approaching the animal-other through "a visceral and empathetic understanding" (315).

For Bentham the question is not whether animals can think or speak, or in Derrida's words, not to know "whether animals are of the type *zōon logon echon,* whether they *can* speak or reason thanks to that *capacity* or that *attribute* of the *logos,* the *can-have* [pouvoir-avoir] of the *logos,* the aptitude for the *logos*" (Derrida 27). The vital thing would be, as Bentham asked, "to know whether they *can suffer*" (Derrida 27). It is hard to give a negative answer to this question, nor is it easy, once the undeniable response is given, to raise other questions based on the hierarchical and dichotomy-oriented structures. Such an answer "which precedes all other questions" (28) and which suddenly leaves the human being face to face with the animal-other in their similarity, can also give way to a possibility for an ethics based on compassion,[7] that is suffering with them. Then the question to ask is not whether the border between the animal and the human is passable or not ("he crossed an invisible borderline"), it is whether we are prepared to give up the privileged ontological status which we accorded ourselves. Welcoming the idea that animals can suffer too, are we ready to sympathise with them, to hear and to listen to them? Is it possible to welcome a philosophy of difference based on similarity, commonness and sharing?

Conclusion

Grizzly Man is films within a film and narrations within a narration. Perhaps Ames is right in claiming that even though at first glance, it seems to be a film about Treadwell, it is more a film about Herzog's statement about nature, about life and death (256). Through his ever-present voice over, editing and the sequence of events, we are given a representation

---

7   Etymologically compassion means "to suffer (*passion*) with, together (*com*)."

of Treadwell and his childish relationship to the animal-other, which can and should occur only in feral tales. However, in real life, as it is implied by Herzog, it may only cause the irreversible damage done to the animals. Though "we may agree with" Herzog at this particular point, that is, Treadwell might have caused such damage, though unintentionally, his attitude, that is his mimetic performance, is an example of loosening the seemingly impassable border between the human-animal and the animal, a border which also positions and re-positions the animal-other and nature as a whole at a distance. I would not complain about this distance if it were a spatial one, and as such enabled us only to look at the animal-other from the other side of the border, without damaging them, without causing them to suffer. However, paradoxically enough, the same distance, perhaps one may say the theoretical[8] distance, enables us to objectify, to use, to manipulate the animal. It is this distance itself, which brings the animal-other closer to us for our own use.

We are also told that Treadwell invented a story and a persona, and it is implied that behind his desire to be with-animals and his longing for becoming-like-a-bear may lie his desire to be a celebrity. I do not think we are in a position to judge his sincerity. There is, however, another way of looking at it: he might have rejected the life given to him and created another "identity." Only in doing so he might have pursued his "happiness" as a person who has indisputable control over his "identity," an identity that is in the state of becoming. As Hannah Arendt put it:

> [...] whoever consciously aims at being "essential," at leaving behind a story and an identity which will win "immortal fame," must not only risk his life but expressly choose, as Achilles did, a short life and premature death. Only a man who does not survive his one supreme act remains the indisputable master of his identity and possible greatness, because he withdraws into death from the possible consequences and continuation of what he began (Arendt 193–194).

Treadwell was not a hero like Achilles and will never become one; he may have withdrawn from the consequences of what he did, and for some those consequences were not in themselves of great importance. They did though include having a film made about him which raised some questions about identity, subjectivity and the dissolution of subjectivity, questions that

---

8   The Greek *theoria* meant contemplation, looking at, speculation, thing looked at.

might also be raised by the lives of other non-heroic people whose *names* can easily be forgotten. Derrida might be right in claiming that nature and animality are born not only out of muteness, but also out of the wound without a name: "that of having *been given a name*," (Derrida 19) but the name *Grizzly Man*, which suggests human-animality, and which blurs the boundary between the two, is certainly not mute. This is something for which we have Herzog to thank.

Works Cited

Agamben, Giorgio. *The Open: Man and Animal*. Translated by Kevin Attell. Stanford, CA: Stanford University Press, 2004.

Ames, Eric. *Ferocious Reality: Documentary According to Werner Herzog*. Minneapolis: University of Minnesota Press, 2012.

Arendt, Hannah. *The Human Condition*. Chicago: University of Chicago Press, 1958.

Aristotle. *History of Animals*. Cambridge, MA: Harvard University Press, 2014.

Bentham, Jeremy. *The Principles of Morals and Legislation*. Buffalo, NY: Prometheus Books, 1988

Birke, Lynda and Luciana Parisi. "Animals, Becoming." *Animal Others: On Ethics, Ontology and Animal Life*, edited by H. Peter Steeves. New York: State University of New York Press, 1999.

Blumenberg, Hans. *Begriffe in Geschichten*. Frankfurt: Suhrkamp Verlag, 1998.

Blumenberg, Hans. *Work on Myth*. Translated by Robert Wallace. Cambridge; London: MIT Press, 1985.

Brinks, Ellen. "Uncovering the Child in Timothy Treadwell's Feral Tale." *The Lion and the Unicorn*, vol. 32, 2008, pp. 304–323.

Deleuze, Gilles and Felix Guattari. *A Thousand Plateaus: Capitalism and Schizophrenia*. Translated by Brian Massumi. Minneapolis; London: University of Minneapolis Press, 2007.

Derrida, Jacques. *The Animal That Therefore I am*. Translated by David Wills. New York: Fordham University Press, 2008.

Grey, John. "'Use Them at Our Pleasure:' Spinoza on Animal Ethics." *History of Philosophy Quarterly*, vol. 30, no. 4, 2013, pp. 367–388.

Heidegger, Martin. *Being and Time*. Translated by John Macquarrie and Edward Robinson. Oxford: Basil Blackwell, 1962.

Heidegger, Martin. *Poetry, Language, Thought*. Translated by A. Hofstadter. New York: Harper and Row, 1971.

Heidegger, Martin. *The Fundamental Concepts of Metaphysics: World, Finitude, Solitude*. Translated by William McNeill and Nicholas Walker. Bloomington and Indiana: Indiana University Press, 1995.

Jeong, Seung-Hoon and Dudley Andrew. "Grizzly Ghost: Herzog, Bazin and the Cinematical Animal." *Screen*, vol. 49, no. 1, 2008, pp. 1–12.

Lovejoy, Arthur O. *The Great Chain of Beings: A Study of the History of an Idea*. New Brunswick; London: Transaction Publishers, 2009.

Montaigne, Michel de. *An Apology for Raymond Sebond*. Translated by M. A. Screech. London: Penguin, 1993.

Nietzsche, Friedrich. *On the Genealogy of Morality*. Translated by Carole Diethe. Cambridge: Cambridge University Press, 2007.

Nietzsche, Friedrich. *Untimely Meditations*. Translated by R. J. Hollingdale. Cambridge: Cambridge University Press, 1997.

Silverman, Kaja. "All Things Shining." *Loss: The Politics of Mourning*, edited by David L. Eng and David Kazanjan. Berkeley: University of California, 2003.

Singer, Peter. "All Animals are Equal." *Applied Ethics*, edited by Peter Singer. Oxford: Oxford University Press, 2011.

Singer, Peter. "Animal Liberation or Animal Rights?" *The Monist*, vol. 70, no. 1, 1987, pp. 3–14.

Spinoza, Benedict de. *Ethics*. Translated by Edwin Curley. London: Penguin, 1996.

White, Lynn, Jr. "The Historical Roots of Our Ecological Crisis." *Science*, vol. 115, no. 3767, 1967, pp. 1203–7.

Wilson, Margaret. " 'For they do not agree in nature with us:' Spinoza on the lower animals." *New Essays on the Rationalists*, edited by R. j. Gennaro and C. Huenemann. Princeton, NJ: Princeton University Press, 1999.

Canan Şavkay

The Precarious Lives of Cats in Doris Lessing's *On Cats*

Lessing's *On Cats,* first published in 1983, describes the writer's personal experience with a variety of cats, some her own, some stray, over a long span of time. The book as a whole emphasizes the precarious position cats occupy as companion animals, because as such, they are positioned between the human world and nature. This in-between position renders them extremely vulnerable, as it makes them not only physically, but also emotionally dependent on humans. The book's focal point is exclusively cats and their precarious position, so much so that the whole human world recedes into the background. The details of the cats' lives, such as their rivalries, preferences, matings, births and their maternal relation to their kittens reveal the narrator's profound love and admiration for these feline companions, yet one of the major emotions the book also evokes and that stands out is the narrator's sense of guilt towards cats. Not a personal guilt, but a general guilt that calls the reader up to a sense of responsibility. As the narrator states, "Knowing cats, a lifetime of cats, what is left is a sediment of sorrow quite different from that due to humans: compounded of pain for their helplessness, of guilt on behalf of us all" (215).

The narrator's sense of guilt evokes a profound feeling of compassion, making her adopt a non-anthropocentric point of view and focus on the lives of cats. Together with this non-anthropocentric perspective, the narrator at the same time subverts the humanist concept of animals as humanity's inferior other. Describing the traditional humanist notion of Man, Val Plumwood contends that, "What is taken to be authentically and characteristically human... is *not* to be found in what is shared with the natural and animal (e.g., the body, sexuality, reproduction, emotionality, the senses, agency) but in what is thought to separate and distinguish them - especially reason and its offshoots (11).

In contrast to this humanist view, Lessing makes her book's focal point those aspects which anthropocentrism excludes. Contrary to the common view which equates the human gaze with power, Lessing refrains from using a language of domination and control and instead attempts to reach out towards the alterity of the cat. As Carol J. Adams contends, "Within patriarchal culture, constituting oneself as a subject involves having an object who is looked at" (15). Consequently, it is the "culturally established *to-be-looked-at-ness* of animals" (18) that justifies cruelty against them. Lessing's gaze, by contrast, tries to bridge the gap between herself and the alterity of the animal. As she significantly writes in the last sentence of her book, "Human and cat, we try to transcend what separates us" (245).

Lessing's attitude throughout the book is clearly relational and consequently opposed to the humanist prioritization of autonomy. Jean Keller maintains that, "Autonomy has been thought of as the pinnacle of human achievement, ... *the* mark of moral maturity. Yet the capacity to form and maintain relationships, which has received little attention in the Western philosophical tradition, is arguably just as much of an achievement as autonomy" (154). The very last scene of the book which describes Lessing sitting beside her cat underscores the narrative's purpose of subverting the traditional approach towards animals, for this final portrait of her and the cat El Magnifico underscores Lessing's emphasis on relation: "When I sit down to be with him, it means slowing myself down, getting rid of the fret and the urgency. When I do this – and he must be in the right mood too, not in pain or restless – then he subtly lets me know he understands I am trying to reach him" (245).

This meeting between human and cat brings to mind Derrida's critique of philosophy's long-standing view of animals as inferior beings. As Derrida points out, philosophers have for a long time "neither wanted nor had the capacity to draw any systematic consequence from the fact that an animal could, facing them, look at them... without a word, *address them*. They have taken no account of the fact that what they call 'animal' could *look at* them, and *address* them from down there, from a wholly other origin" (13). Derrida's statement turns upside down the conventional encounter with the animal by describing a situation in which he himself is followed into his bathroom by his cat who looks up at him. Being naked, Derrida expresses his shame in front of the cat and then delves into a discourse that explores our relation to animals. Despite the similarity between Derrida's and Lessing's encounter with their cats, one profound difference prevails between these two encounters: In Derrida's case it is he himself who is addressed by his cat, whereas in Lessing's case, it is she who initiates the encounter when she sits down beside the cat, emphasizing her willingness to bridge the gap. The cat, in turn, responds by letting her know that he understands her desire to reach him.

The fact that Lessing ends the book with the cat's response is highly significant, for, as Derrida points out,

> All the philosophers we will investigate (from Aristotle to Lacan, and including Descartes, Kant, Heidegger, and Levinas), all of them say the same thing: the animal is deprived of language. Or, more precisely, of response, of a response that could be precisely and rigorously distinguished from a reaction; of the right and power to 'respond,' and hence of so many other things that would be proper for man (32).

By acknowledging that her cat possesses the ability to understand her desire to reach him, Lessing endows the cat with depth of mind and thus with an inner life. Underscoring her cat's capacity to respond, the narrator recognizes El Magnifico's interiority and consciousness, thereby revealing a high respect for the animal's alterity. However, it should be noted that the verb 'to respond,' used by Derrida in the above quotation, is not used in the sense of 'react,' but according to Lacan's understanding of this term. Derrida points out that although Lacan acknowledges the existence of a language system in bees, he nevertheless believes that bees do not actually respond when they receive a message, but merely react to it according to "a fixed program" (123). As such, Lacan appears to be "deeply embedded... in the Cartesian tradition's conceptualization of the animal as something that can only 'react' and not 'respond'" (Wolfe, *Animal Rites* 74).

In contrast to Lacan's view on animals, El Magnifico actually responds to Lessing's attempt to bridge the gap and this attempt to relate is an overt expression of respect for the Other. According to Donna Haraway, respect is a precondition for an authentic encounter between species, pointing out that the word 'respect' derives etymologically from 'respecere,' meaning "seeing again" and "To hold in regard, to respond, to look back reciprocally" (19). Haraway admits that despite her admiration for Derrida's overall work, she is disappointed in him, because "he failed a simple obligation of companion species; he did not become curious about what the cat might actually doing, feeling, thinking, ... What happened that morning was, to me, shocking *because* of what I knew this philosopher can do. Incurious, he missed a possible invitation" (20). Hence, what sets off Lessing's encounter from Derrida's is the fact that Lessing is actually curious about the alterity of the cat and consequently concentrates on the cat's life which is so different from the life of a human being. Derrida, by contrast, digresses away from the cat and loses himself in a discourse on philosophy. Maintaining that Derrida's critique of humanism eventually succumbs to humanist values, Susan Fraiman notes, "True that Derrida's cat is accorded the power of the gaze: the singular, discerning 'point of view' traditionally tied to cognition and reserved for humans. Yet the bathroom transaction overall... leaves intact the old rationalist hierarchy valuing vision/mind/cognition over touch/body/emotion" (96).

Lessing, by contrast, deliberately directs her readers' attention towards the tangible and emotional experience of cats and thereby subverts the hierarchal relation between reason and the body together with its emotions. Evoking feelings of love and compassion, Lessing goes contrary to animal rights advocates such as Cary Wolfe who claim that the struggle for animal rights "has nothing to do with whether you like animals" (*Animal Rites* 7). Pointing out that it is mainly the male animal rights theorists who reject emotion, Josephine Donovan contends, "Women animal rights theorists seem, indeed, to have developed more of a sense of emotional bonding with animals as the basis for their theory than is evident in the male literature" (168).

Although Lessing displays emotions in her book, such as love, compassion or guilt, it is nevertheless very interesting to note that she at the same time refrains from indulging in the expression of her own emotions. As Ellen Peel observes, Lessing's "nonfictional perspective... turns the focus away from the author herself" (3), because an overt display of emotion is always in danger of drawing the reader's attention away from the cat and towards the narrator. Consequently, she takes care not to fall back on a human-centered exposition. As Cary Wolfe notes, this is always a danger when writing about animals: "Just because we direct our attention to the study of nonhuman animals, and even if we do so with the aim of exposing how they have been misunderstood and exploited, that does not mean that we are not continuing to be humanist – and therefore, by definition, anthropocentric" (*Posthumanism* 99).

The following scene perfectly illustrates how Lessing evokes feelings of compassion in the reader while evading the depiction of her own emotions. Lessing remembers a scene from her youth in Africa when a former cat of theirs who had gone stray returns pregnant, but remains completely shy of them, only accepting their food as long as the humans do not come close to her. Then one night during a heavy rainy storm the cat reappears desperately crying for help. The members of the household follow the cat through the rain until they reach the entrance of an abandoned shaft and as it is too dangerous to enter the shaft in the dark, they return home. As soon as it gets light, they return to the shaft looking for the cat and find her buried in mud that had slid down the walls of the shaft. The narrator's position in the depiction of the rescue scene is highly significant, for she writes:

> She had come up to the house so that we could rescue the kittens. She had been frightened to come near the house because of the hostility of the other cats and the dogs, perhaps because she now feared us, but she had overcome her fear to get help for the kittens. But she had not been given help. She must have lost all hope that night, as the rain lashed down, as earth slid in all around her, as the water crept up behind her in the dark collapsing tunnel. But she had fed the kittens, and they were alive (165).

It is significant to note that the narrative tone does not indulge in a description of the rescuers' emotional response in this highly melodramatic scene. When they follow the cat to the abandoned shaft, light their torches into the dark and realize how dangerous the entry into the shaft would be, the narrator merely states that they returned home and the following statement is the only description of the feelings of the people who tried to rescue the cat and her kittens during the heavy rain: "But we slept badly, thinking of the poor cat, and got up at five with the first light" (163). Another very important feature which marks this passage is the consistent use of the pronoun 'we' each time the human rescuers are mentioned. Nowhere does the narrator explicitly give information concerning who 'we' refers to and the reader has not even a clue concerning the number of human beings this pronoun contains. By placing her own emotions into the background, Lessing directs the reader's attention towards the cat's experience.

As already pointed out, the narrative draws attention to the ambivalent position of cats who, as companion animals, occupy a place between nature and humans. In order to emphasize their ambivalent position, the book does not begin with the book's central theme, namely cats, but with the narrator's relation to the natural world, underscored in her encounter with the hawks. In the hawks' case, however, the encounter is not marked by an attempt to reach out toward the other. When the narrator looks into the eye of the hawk who circles the air, her gaze is just as cold as that of the predator: "Hundreds of feet up, a dozen birds circled, all eyeing the field for small movement of mouse, birds, or mole. You would choose one, straight overhead perhaps; perhaps for a moment fancy an exchanged glance eye to eye: the cold staring eye of the bird into coldly curious human eye" (3–4). Although Lessing's gaze expresses her interest in the hawks, she still does not reveal the closeness and warmth that characterizes her relation with El Magnifico.

The description of the hawks actually serves as a prelude to the portrait of the cats in the book. The narrator explains that because of the huge number of hawks, nobody usually bothered to shoot them, unless there was reason for hot anger. She says, "So the hawks were not shot. Unless in rage. I remember, when that kitten vanished mewing into the sky in the hawk's claws, my mother exploded the shotgun after it. Futilely of course" (6). The relation between hawks and cats introduces the theme of the cats' vulnerability, because the first time cats are mentioned in this book, they are portrayed as prey (5). The fact that the first cat described to be harmed is a kitten evokes a sense of compassion in the reader, thereby emphasizing the cats' need for human protection. The hawks, snakes and other wild-life mentioned by the narrator are self-sustaining, yet cats as companion animals depend on humans and not only on a physical, but also on an emotional plane.

However, it is not only cats, but also humans, who are portrayed to be threatened by the surrounding wildlife. The narrator remembers how their farm used to be beleaguered by cobras, black mambas and various sorts of adders (10). She further mentions how her brother was once attacked by a snake which is known to blind its enemies by spitting into their eyes. The narrator only factually mentions that her brother's "sight was saved by an African who used bush medicine" (10), without describing the panic and distress the snake's attack must have initially caused. The same non-emotional attitude is adopted in the narrator's own case when she mentions how she was once nearly bitten by a poisonous snake. The whole incident is described in only one sentence: "Once I nearly picked a night-adder up, mistaking it for a skein of darning wool. But it feared me first, and its hissing saved us both: I ran; and it got away" (10). In both cases the descriptions are rendered as a matter of fact and emotional reactions concerning the confrontation with the snakes are absent.

However, when it comes to cats, we are made to feel for them. Of course, these cats are indeed harmed by the snakes, yet this is not the only reason why we feel sympathy for them. The narrator writes, "Flashes of memory, stories without beginnings or ends. What happened to the cat who lay stretched out on my mother's bed, miaowing with pain, its eyes swollen up from a spitting snake? Or the cat who came crying into the house, her belly dragging to the ground with unused milk?" (12). The crucial point in the case of the cats is the way they are depicted in need of humans. Emphasizing the importance of acknowledging our own vulnerability, James Stanescu claims that, "It is our very ability to be wounded, our very dependency, that brings us together" (578) and this is exactly Lessing's concern. Although the human world is also surrounded by wild animals, the cats in the book appear to be much more in need of care than the humans. The humans possess guns with which they shoot unwanted wild-life and therefore appear to be much more in power and control than the cats. It is therefore the emphasis on their vulnerability which draws a clear line of demarcation between domestic cats and wild animals. The narrator admits that whereas the people on the farm cared for the domestic cats, they were rather hostile towards the wild cats. She says, "We hated wild cats, which spat and clawed and hissed and hated us" (8). It seems here that Lessing refers to her former self when she expresses her hatred, for the above statement rather appears like a consciously adopted ironic stance. The wild cats are clearly put into the position of an aggressive other and human hostility is merely a reaction to the wild cats' violent behavior.

It is significant to note how the whole tone changes as soon as the narrator realizes that the wild cat she has just shot is actually not wild, but Minnie, "an enchanting pet from two years before who had disappeared – taken, we thought, by a hawk or an owl" (8). The relation here between nature and the human world is marked by the distinction between 'us' and 'them,' for as soon as the cat adopts a name, the killing changes its meaning. As the narrator admits, "Wild cats mated with our cats, lured peaceful domestic pussies off to dangerous lives in the bush for which, we were convinced, they were not fitted. Wild cats brought into dubious question the status of our comfortable beasts" (7).

However, the fact that domestic cats are clearly distinguished from wild cats does not mean that humans do not kill domestic cats as well. In view of cats' over-productive fertility, humans in the book take on the role of their natural enemy by acting out nature's role as regulator of populations through selection. As the narrator notes, "A litter of six kittens in a warm basket in a town house can be seen, perhaps, as eagle and hawk fodder in the wrong place? But then, how inflexible is nature, how unpliable: if cats have been the friends of man for so many centuries, could nature not have adapted itself, just a little, away from the formula: five or six kittens to a litter, four times a year?" (28).

Due to the absence of natural enemies, the function of regulating the 'right' number of cats has to be undertaken by humans. The narrator reports that during her childhood it used to be her mother who killed the kittens until she felt emotionally drained and started to refuse to kill any more of them. Her mother's refusal, however, leads to the growth of the feline population, so much so that eventually the whole farm is festered with them. As the narrator explains, "There was nothing to prevent us, within a few weeks, from becoming the battleground for a hundred cats" (15). Consequently, she and her father have to take on the task of putting the cats to death and after the slaughter, they are both so upset that they decide this must never happen again, implying that in the future they will have to take measures beforehand and continue to kill some of the kittens.

It is specifically through this point that the narrator emphasizes the ambivalent relation between humans and cats. While her non-anthropocentric perspective and desire to reach out underscore Lessing's critical engagement with humanist assumptions, such as the centrality of the human subject, she also feels forced to act in the role of nature, deciding over the fate of individual cats. As such, she underscores the problematic relation between cat and human, for no matter how much she adopts a non-anthropocentric stance and tries to reach out towards the alterity of the cat, the fact remains that the regulation of the feline population reinstates the humanistic hierarchical relation between human and cat. At this point it might be helpful to cite Rosi Braidotti's definition of the posthuman in order to better understand this issue. Braidotti states that, "The posthuman in the sense of post-anthropocentrism displaces the dialectical scheme of opposition, replacing well-established dualisms with the recognition of deep zoe-egalitarianism between humans and animals. The vitality of their bond is based on sharing this planet, territory or environment on terms that are no longer so clearly hierarchical, nor self-evident" (71).

Braidotti's emphasis on posthumanism's interrogation of the hierarchy between human and animal is crucial at this point, for instead of focusing on our differences, it underscores what we have in common, such as the fact that we share the same planet and are all part of one and the same nature. When Lessing writes about the killing of kittens or the need to have her cats operated, she does not enjoy these acts; neither does she take these issues lightly by putting all the blame on nature. On the contrary, interfering with the lives of cats leads to her feelings of guilt. In other words, she does not justify her actions through humanist assumptions, placing the human above the animal. It is significant to note that the killing of the cats on the farm, for example, is neither done in cold blood, nor is it done with pleasure. Its cause is nature's abundant procreativity which gives life but remains indifferent to the death of individual members of any species. The humans are not happy at all to act in the role of nature, for as the narrator points out, "it was not my father who drowned the kittens, shot the snake, killed the diseased fowl, or burned sulphur in the white ant nest: my father liked white ants, enjoyed watching them" (14). Her mother used to accomplish this task, because "she was one of that part of humankind *which understands how things work*; and works with them. A grim enough role" (13).

Her mother understands much better nature's indifference towards the individual members of any species and acts accordingly. Lessing, by contrast, indeed feels pity and compassion and extends her love and care to them. The following passage clearly describes her close emotional bond with a cat. Lessing writes,

> After a certain age – and for some of us that can be very young – there are no new people, beasts, dreams, faces, events: it has all happened before, they have appeared before, masked differently, wearing different clothes, another

nationality, another colour; but the same, the same, and everything is an echo and a repetition; and there is no grief even that it is not a recurrence of something long out of memory that expresses itself in unbelievable anguish, days of tears, loneliness, knowledge of betrayal and all for a small, thin, dying cat (20).

This small, thin, dying cat had been a close companion during a period of illness when she was a child. "The cat, a bluish-grey Persian, arrived purring on my bed, and settled down to share my sickness, my food, my pillow, my sleep" (21). She remembers the cat's warmth as she snuggled up against her, while the room's air was freezing and the linen of her bed felt cold to her touch. However, this cat later falls into a tub filled with hot water and although it is rescued and given medical treatment, it does not survive the accident. Obviously, the loss of this cat must have been very painful to the narrator, because she states that this cat became so unique to her that for years she compared all other cats with this one. It is therefore even more striking that her description of the cat's death is almost devoid of her own feelings: "For a week she lay in my arms purring, purring, in a rough trembling hoarse little voice that became weaker, then was silent; licked my hand; opened enormous green eyes when I called her name and besought her to live; closed them, died" (22). Avoiding to indulge in her own sorrow, she directs the reader's attention away from herself, evoking feelings of sympathy for the cat and the phrase quoted above, "and all for a small, thin, dying cat" is clearly ironic, as it counterbalances her view of the cat as unique as opposed to nature's indifference.

The compassion she feels for the cat characterizes her sense of responsibility and guilt in the face of the inability not to be sufficiently able to protect a cat from suffering. She tells how as a three-year old child she brought home a starving kitten and against the protest of her parents insisted on keeping the cat. Eventually her parents give in:

They washed it in permanganate because it was filthy; and thereafter it slept on my bed. I would not let it be taken away from me. But of course it must have been, for the family left Persia, and the cat stayed behind. Or perhaps it died. Perhaps – but how do I know? Anyway, somewhere back there, a very small girl had fought for and won a cat who kept her days and nights company; and then she lost it (19–20).

The awareness of betrayal comes to her much later and it is the sense of responsibility for the other who in his or her vulnerability is betrayed that leads to her sense of guilt. This sense of guilt comes also to the fore when the question of having cats operated arises. Lessing writes that after the operation, the cat "looked at me with enormous dark shocked eyes. She had been betrayed and she knew it. She had been sold out by a friend, the person who fed her, protected her, whose bed she slept on. A terrible thing had been done to her. I couldn't bear to look at her eyes" (79). Another such example is the scene in which she looks at her cat El Magnifico after he has been neutered. She understands what his gaze means, for she says that he "lifted his head and looked at me and never has anything been clearer than that long deep look: You are my friend, and yet you have done this to me" (232–3). She had been initially unwilling to have her cats operated and she only relents when members of the R.S.P.C.A. advise her to do so. Lessing thinks, "Understandably: they have to destroy hundreds of unwanted cats every week – every one of which, I suppose, has been to someone 'Oh what a lovely kitten' – until it grew up" (75–76). What Lessing underscores in the suffering of the cats is their inability to give meaning to the pain, because this aspect turns "that pain and suffering into something uncontrollable and overpowering" (Aaltola 19).

Acknowledging the other's vulnerability requires empathy and, as Cora Diamond points out:

> There is not first an establishing that animals have characteristics that we share, and that are the basis for allowing animals to count as possible victims of injustice. Rather, there is a kind of response in the face of what is done to them: a pain and revulsion that requires for its expression the language of injustice, a pain and revulsion felt as akin to that at the exercise of power without curb over vulnerable human beings. This pain or revulsion or horror at what is done to animals has internal to it a way of understanding their lives, the reality of those lives (139).

Diamond's emphasis on empathy is to be found in Lessing's representation of cats. The narrator's focus on cats as both physically and emotionally dependent on humans gives rise to the question of ethics, because human beings in their more autonomous position have the choice of either responding to or ignoring the suffering of others. The following example perfectly explains the underlying causes of indifference to others' suffering. Lessing remembers how a stray cat, who obviously wanted to be adopted by the people who fed it, used to visit the building where she lived. As the season got colder, the cat began to sleep inside the building and when the cold got worse, some of the inhabitants took it into their flat overnight, until the caretaker reported the cat to the council and it was taken and killed. The narrator's brief explanation for the caretaker's motive is full of insight: "One night, the hours of waiting for the door to be opened had proved too long, and it had made a mess on a landing. The caretaker was not going to put up with that, he said. Bad enough clearing up after us lot, he wasn't going to clean up after cats as well" (39–40). In this brief passage the narrator exposes the resentment of the caretaker who obviously considers his position to be below that of the inhabitants and hence, bears a grudge. Regarding the cat as inferior to him, the caretaker vents off his frustration by asserting himself in the face of a defenseless cat.

The caretaker's disregard for the cat's life underscores Lessing's concern with the nature of care, for it is this caring stance that marks her relation to cats throughout the book. This question of care, however, points at a further problem in the book, namely the question to whom we give precedence, for when we care and cherish, we may sometimes do so at the expense of another. For example, cats are predators and even domestic cats love to prey on birds and when Lessing describes her cat catching birds, she feels resentment for indirectly contributing to the killing of birds. She scolds her cat and even rescues some of the birds from its claws, yet most of the time the cat ends up killing the birds which it not even cares to eat. When Lessing reminisces about a workman she once asked to trim a tree in her garden, she underscores that care also requires a choice of priority, for the workman is extremely upset with people who want him to cut perfectly healthy trees which provide a home for birds. Lessing thinks, "For the tree man, trees and birds, a unit, a sacred unit to be given preference, I should imagine, over human beings, if he had the decision. As for cats, he'd get rid of them all" (112).

Lessing's priority is without doubt cats and although she describes the love and care she extends towards them, she is also very honest and does not hide the fact that she sometimes found herself forced to kill cats. This killing is not confined to the slaughter of the cats on the African farm; she also talks about how she and a few others with whom she temporarily shared a country house once killed four newly-born kittens. They do so because they believe the mother cat has already given birth to too many kittens and it had been difficult enough for them to find new homes. Lessing's description of this scene is very interesting:

> So we did. It was horrible. Then two of us went out into the long field in the dark with torches and we dug a hole while the rain fell steadily, and we buried the four dead kittens and we swore and cursed at nature, at each other, and at life; and then we went back to the long quiet farm room where the fire burned, and there was black cat on a clean blanket, a pretty, proud cat with two kittens – civilization had triumphed again (140–1).

Despite her confession to have killed cats, Lessing stands out in the way she expresses a sincere care for cats. The overall role she adopts in relation to them is definitely maternal, for she not only feeds, but also nurses them in their sickness. Judith Kegan Gardiner maintains that Lessing's preoccupation with mothering and care in *On Cats* reveals her concern with her own maternal function. Gardiner points out that "It is the only one of her books dedicated to the daughter she left behind in Africa when she moved to England with her young son. In this light, the book's many incidents in which Lessing faithfully feeds and nurses sick cats appear as covert proofs that she is really a good mother after all" (121). In view of the profound way this book deals with questions pertaining to our relation with animals, it is highly doubtful whether Lessing's actual purpose of writing this book was to present herself as a good mother. However, Gardiner is certainly right when she points out that the book's central concern actually revolves around the role of the maternal, because it is through the maternal role humans play that Lessing underscores the precariousness of cats as companion species. When black cat, for example, gets ill and is about to die, Lessing does almost everything in her power to bring her back to life, even though she is perfectly aware that the cat wants to die (88). Rufus, a stray cat who has been abandoned by the people who looked after him and as a result lost his health on the streets, is another cat who is looked well by her. She also tenderly takes care of El Magnifico whose leg needs amputation after being diagnosed with cancer. The portrait of El Magnifico after the operation is very touching, as he does not understand why his leg has been taken off.

The maternal role towards animals underscores the problematic aspect of our relation with animals, for as companion species cats have lost their independence and become reliant on humans. This has deeply affected their psychology and disturbed the maternal instinct in some of the mother cats, for being turned into immature beings, mother cats might no longer follow their instincts.

The first cat Lessing acquires in London and refers to as the black-and-white cat insists on staying close to the humans during her labor. The next mother cat whose birth is described likewise seeks the company of humans and after she has her litter, the mother just abandons her kittens, going down to the kitchen in order to be close to the humans. For this she is heavily scolded by the narrator who states, "She had understood, by morning, that she was responsible for those kittens. But left to herself, that great Mother, nature, notwithstanding, she would have let them starve" (63). Although her other cat, the one she calls black cat, turns out to be a good mother to her kittens, black cat also insists on receiving human comfort during labor. As such, these mother cats are all portrayed as rather immature and it is this feature which emphasizes their vulnerability.

In view of their vulnerability, the narrator reacts with a sense of responsibility and care. Her concern is clearly ethical, for she provides a portrait of the animal as other without trying to render it as inferior. Taken as a whole, the book is a declaration of love for cats, for the narrator's focus on the details of the cats' physical beauty is clear proof of her appreciation. The following description perfectly illustrates this love for detail when Lessing describes grey cat:

> deliberate, she would crouch and fascinate me with her eyes. I stared into them, almond-shaped in their fine outline of dark pencil, around which was a second pencilling of cream. Under each, a brush stroke of dark. Green, green eyes; but in shadow, a dark smoky gold – a dark-eyed cat. But in the light, green, a clear cool emerald. Behind the transparent globes of the eyeball, slices of veined gleaming butterfly wing. Wings like jewels – the essence of wing (71).

Passages such as these underscore the reason for adopting cats as companions, because their grace and beauty enrich our lives and make us stand in awe in front of nature. Although Lessing interrogates humanist concepts and draws attention to our guilt for having interfered with cats' lives, the book is pervaded by a profound love and admiration for our feline companions and a plea to take them seriously. The narrative reminds us to observe cats carefully and see them as gifts of nature. Contemplating on cats, Lessing writes,

What a luxury a cat is, the moments of shocking and startling pleasure in a day, the feel of the beast, the soft sleekness under your palm, the warmth when you wake on a cold night, the grace and charm even in a quite ordinary workaday puss. Cat walks across your room, and in that lonely stalk you see leopard or even panther, or it turns its head to acknowledge you and the yellow blaze of those eyes tells you what an exotic visitor you have here, in this household friend, the cat who purrs as you stroke, or rub his chin, or scratch his head (241–2).

Lessing's attitude throughout the book is clearly relational and consequently opposed to the humanist prioritization of autonomy. Interestingly, Lessing ignores the question of human autonomy and instead directs the reader's attention towards responsibility and appreciation for the animal's alterity. Representing the tangible aspect of cats' lives, she does not put them into the position of humanity's inferior other, but establishes an emotional bond between cat and human. As such, she subverts the humanist concept of Man as a rational and autonomous being and replaces it with a focus on our relational capacities. Lessing's representation of cats is therefore an indirect interrogation of humanist concepts. It is a very emotional book evoking love and appreciation in the reader, while also drawing attention to the vulnerable position of our companions and this is why the underlying emotion throughout the book is a sense of guilt.

Works Cited

Aaltola, Elisa. *Animal Suffering: Philosophy and Culture.* Palgrave Macmillan, 2012.

Adams, Carol J. *Neither Man Nor Beast: Feminism and the Defense of Animals.* Bloomsbury, 2018.

Braidotti, Rosi. *The Posthuman.* Polity Press, 2013.

Derrida, Jacques. *The Animal That Therefore I Am.* Edited by Marie-Luise Mallet. Fordham, 2008.

Diamond, Cora. "Injustice and Animals." *Slow Cures and Bad Philosophers: Essays on Wittgenstein, Medicine, and Bioethics*, edited by Carl Elliott. Duke UP, 2001, pp. 118–148.

Donovan, Josephine. "Animal Rights and Feminist Theory." *Ecofeminism: Women, Animals, Nature,* edited by Greta Gaard. Temple UP, Philadelphia, 1993, pp. 167–194.

Fraiman, Susan. "Pussy Panic versus Liking Animals: Tracking Gender in Animal Studies." *Critical Inquiry*, vol. 39, no. 1, Autumn 2002, pp. 89–115.

Gardiner, Judith Kegan. "Gender, Values, and Lessing's Cats." *Tulsa Studies in Women's Literature*, vol. 3, no. 1/2, Spring-Autumn 1984, pp. 111–124.

Haraway, Donna, J. *When Species Meet*. University of Minnesota Press, 2008.

Keller, Jean. "Autonomy, Rationality, and Feminist Ethics." *Hypatia*, vol. 12, no. 2, Spring 1997, pp. 152–164.

Lessing, Doris. *On Cats*. HarperCollins, 2008.

Peel, Ellen. "The Self Is Always an Other: Going the Long Way Home to Autobiography." *Twentieth Century Literature*, vol. 35, no. 1, Spring 1989, pp. 1–16.

Plumwood, Val. "Nature, Self and Gender: Feminism, Environmental Philosophy, and the Critique of Rationalism." *Hypatia*, vol. 6, no. 1, Spring 1991, pp. 3–27.

Stanescu, James. "Judith Butler, Mourning, and the Precarious Lives of Animals." *Hypatia*, vol. 27, no. 3, Summer 2012, pp. 567–582.

Wolfe, Cary. *Animal Rites: American Culture, the Discourse of Species, and Posthumanist Theory*. University of Chicago Press, 2003.

Wolfe, Cary. *What Is Posthumanism?* University of Minnesota Press, 2010.

Ferdi Çetin

Decentering the Human on Stage: *Neither* as Posthumanist Opera

New connections between the subject and his/her relation to nature need to be considered even to begin to comment on a new notion of subject in theater with fresh references to posthumanism. I shall start, therefore, by focusing on the pronoun we use to identify the subject, nature and the beings either human or animal to show our conventional relationship with them. I start using "he" or "she" for the subject and I can use "it" for nature. Even the choice of a single subject or object pronoun gives me enough idea to start a discussion about previously unchallenged norms. In his book *Humankind: Solidarity with Nonhuman People*, Professor Timothy Morton explains in detail this issue of pronoun:

> There is no pronoun entirely suitable to describe ecological beings. If I call them "I", then I am appropriating them to myself or to some pantheistic or Gaia concept that swallows them all without regard to their specificity. If I call them "you", I differentiate them from the kind of being that I am. If I call them "he" or "she", then I am gendering them according to heteronormative concepts that are untenable on evolutionary terms. If I call them "it", I don't think they are people like me and I'm being blatantly anthropocentric.[1]

Morton shows how problematic it is to use a single pronoun to describe ecological beings. It's not easy to find a solution for this at once as the issue of framing and describing is deeply rooted in Western thinking and seeing. The history starts with the borders which were set between human beings and nature and the battle between them. The "man" has the "obligatory" desire to control nature and this creates the hierarchical mentality. I am repeating, this age-old separation is not an easy matter to handle as the world has been formed accordingly. However, the recent approaches towards nature, culture and the planet bring us the idea of human being not as an omnipresent figure but a weak one who needs assistance and

---

1   Morton, Timothy, Humankind: Solidarity with Nonhuman People, Brooklyn, Verso books, 2017, p.21.

relations. So, we need to reconsider our relationship with nature and the notion of subject as a fully equipped being. I know I have started my discussion on a rather general level but now I have the urgent feeling of creating a link between these newly found arguments and theater. I think the name Gertrude Stein can be a starting point and her ideas about theater fit well to my discussion because she is the one who changed the course of theater by stripping the text of its previously unquestioned burdens which are story, plot and character. First, she focused on writing portraits and short plays which did not have a proper story line and well-established characters. Apart from this, she introduced the idea of landscape with its effect still visible on the contemporary stage. This is how Gertrude Stein described landscape:

> The landscape has its formation and as after all a play has to have formation and be in relation one thing to the other thing and as the story is not the thing as any one is always telling something then the landscape not moving but being always in relation, the trees to the hills the hills to the fields the trees to each other any piece of it to any sky and then any detail to any other detail [...][2]

She created a similarity between a play and a landscape therefore it can be easily said that a play can be formed as a landscape. This concept of play as a landscape introduces the idea of "relation". In conventional theater we see the story and the characters, and these are the most influential tools of the playwright to control the stage. The director is supposed to interpret the world which is created by the playwright. And all the elements on stage are regulated according to this basic idea. This inevitably brings a hierarchical understanding of theater. With the play understood as landscape the hierarchy on stage is demolished and therefore the implications of a relational aesthetics arise. When we have all the concepts of a text without a story and character, a play formed as a landscape and relational aesthetics at hand, we can easily say that the center of the text and stage has been dispersed, the hierarchy has been destroyed and the character, therefore the subject, has been deconstructed. There stands in front of us a "subject" who feels the necessity of building "new" relations with nature, with the environment. I believe that this idea has strong implications for

---

2   Stein, Gertrude, Look at Me Now and Here I Am Writings and Lectures 1909–45, London, Penguin Group, 1990, p.78.

posthumanism as the deconstruction of subject and character gives me the suitable ground on which I can move. This subject who is not at the top of any hierarchical pyramid but among the elements of the scape needs to reevaluate his/her existence. A similar formulation to that of the subject who is not the lord of nature and environment but one of its components in Samuel Beckett's plays. The bodies in his plays are either half visible or completely in darkness. In some of his texts he deconstructs the bodily unity of the characters; they have only the upper parts of their bodies or their arms or only their mouths. And the mouth in darkness can only utter some broken sentences or single words. In a way it can be said that Beckett threw his characters into the void of the stage where they lost their distinct features and lost their identities and unities. At this point we can conclude that reminiscent of Gertrude Stein's quest, Beckett worked on his texts hard enough to rip them of the conventional tools of story and character. The second implication inevitably arises here at this point as Beckett is the modernist playwright who put an end to bodily unity in his texts and on stage. His characters are jailed in a world where they are doomed to act anonymously, and the characters are not even one single step away from the other objects and animals around them. One more time we are face to face with a dispersed idea of the subject who needs the relation with his/her environment to survive. For example, Vladimir and Estragon in *Waiting for Godot* start their journey on a country road with a single tree branch and they do not move nor does a single story develop. The characters are at the center of a landscape where they do not have the power to control. They can only exist without any impact. Their only existence depends on nature.

Aside from Gertrude Stein and Samuel Beckett we have Heiner Goebbels who introduces the term "aesthetics of absence". The term "absence" has strong references to posthumanism and the notion of subject formation. With this third theatrical figure the triangular ground of our discussion will be completed. Heiner Goebbels's name inevitably creates a link between the avant-garde playwright Gertrude Stein's plays in the beginning of the 20th century and the contemporary theatrical works at the end of 20th century. Beginning from his early stage works, Heiner Goebbels has been working on the aesthetics of absence. In other words, his aim can be summarized as to create aesthetics on stage by eliminating previously unquestioned elements of theater from the stage. And to be able to analyze the underlying principles of this notion of aesthetics we always need to go back to the basic terms coined by Gertrude Stein. Keeping in mind Stein's idea of play as landscape, we can move on defining Heiner Goebbels' aesthetics. Heiner Goebbels has adopted the term absence in his first play *Ou Bien le Debarquement Desastreux*. We see a gigantic pyramid on stage and the actor struggles to keep his bodily unity throughout the play. The pyramid swallows the actor at one point, or it jails him at another. The actor loses his unity like Beckettian characters do, and we can see him as much as the huge structure allows. In his other works Goebbels keeps on creating new forms of relationships between humans, animals, robots and machines. In his play titled *Eraritjaritjaka* he introduces two robot machines to an actor who leaves the stage to go on an unguided tour in the city where the venue of each performance is located. The stage stays empty in black and white. In *De Materie* he presents two zeppelins and a flock of sheep to the members of the audience. The spectators are left alone face to face with the wandering sheep. They are made to watch the animals on stage for so long that they leave their conventional ways of seeing aside and they attain new "insights". They also watch a dancing pendulum or flying zeppelins without searching for a fixed meaning.

And the exemplary performance of his aesthetics *Stifters Dinge* is described as a "a composition for five pianos with no pianists, a play with no actors, a performance without performers – one might say a no-man show". The spectators do not meet any performers in the play and there are only musical instruments which make music or noise, three boiling pools and two portraits by celebrated painters. Goebbels uses Adalbert Stifter's texts in this piece, but he does not have aim at staging them. He does not stage a text in the conventional sense, or he does not look for any kind of traditional relationships. The play portrays a kind of untamed garden in which sounds, noises, objects and machines are intertwine and there is not even a single subject. Therefore, the objects gain agency. They are in a sense performative objects which do not need a subject in a phenomenological relationship. In this ecological garden the "man" is not the master. As the human has lost his/her place in the center, the new scape cannot be a place controlled by a human being and so the human may have the potential to restructure his/her relationship with nature and animals.

Once the binary relation has collapsed, there appears new alternatives in terms of subject formation, implicating the term "posthuman condition" coined by the prominent posthumanist scholar Rosi Braidotti. This is how she develops her argument:

> The posthuman predicament is such as to force a displacement of the lines of demarcation between structural differences, or ontological categories, for instance between the organic and the inorganic, the born and the manufactured, flesh and metal, electronic circuits and organic nervous systems.[3]

The main opposition leaves its place to an ambiguity between age-old categories. The previous borders are challenged and demolished and the new "relational subject" who puts the heteronormative and hierarchical classifications aside is born into the Stifter's ecological garden.

When we take into consideration all the names and concepts discussed so far, at this crossing point we can say that by undermining the conventional stage all those artists have helped to create a scape where the human being is not at the center. Take Gertrude Stein for example, she destroys the traditional structure of play text and the character and similarly, Beckett eliminates the fully established story and deterritorializes the characters, and Heiner Goebbels is not interested in characters or plays as he has already started the actor's journey which would end up somewhere out of the stage.

To put it briefly, these writers and directors have all brought the end of character and the center in a play and this inevitably implies more than enough for the idea of "dehumanizing" the stage. Accordingly, the term dehumanizing the stage has something to do with posthumanism as it hints at a new notion of subject and object relation on stage. Now it is high time to imagine how it can be possible to configure these alternative insights realized in a production. We can take Samuel Beckett from the triangular construction and introduce the name Romeo Castellucci.

Samuel Beckett's Opera *Neither*

In 1977 Rome Opera House invited Morton Feldman to compose an opera for the repertoire. Morton Feldman decided to collaborate with

---

3   Rosi Braidotti, The Posthuman, Cambridge, Polity Press, 2013, p.89.

Samuel Beckett for the piece and they started exchanging ideas related to opera and the first thing that they shared was an uneasiness with the form. Beckett expressed that he did not like his words composed and Feldman did not want to use words in his composition. After a while Beckett sent a postcard to Feldman and there was a short poem on it, and the poem had just sixteen lines. This was the beginning of the collaboration and the result was a ground-breaking opera piece which can be classified as anti-opera.

The text which has a fragmented voice travelling among "shadows", "selfness" and "worlds" can be described as one of the most unconventional librettos of opera history. Similarly, Feldman's music is minimalist, and the composition does not have a multi-vocal structure. It was intended only for a soprano. This piece has long been disregarded as it is not theatrical enough and musically not very rich. When Heiner Goebbels became the artistic director of RuhrTriannale in 2013, he invited Italian director Romeo Castellucci to stage an opera for the festival. And this was the beginning for Castellucci's production *Neither*.

Feldman and Beckett's anti-opera *Neither* has become a multidimensional and multidisciplinary work in Castellucci's hands. This fifty-minute solo opera has been designed visually by the director and it has gone further than Feldman and Beckett's version in terms of its multi-layered images and interspecies approach. Contrary to its traditional place, the director has placed the orchestra on stage left in darkness. *Neither* opens with a foreplay in which we watch the famous Schrödinger's cat experiment, which is known as the interpretation of quantum mechanics. In the experiment there is a cat in a closed box and the idea is that it is not possible to exactly know whether the cat is alive or not. Similarly, we see a black box on stage center and the lid of the box is open so the spectators can see two cats, one alive and one death. Once the cover of the box is opened the alive cat jumps on the stage floor and leaves the stage as the dead cat stays in the box. A mother watches the stage with her daughter. When we think about this beginning, we can easily say that the play opens with a clear hint of ambiguity. The very first scene of the play is followed by a scene in which there appears the set of a house with a bedroom, living room and study room. In this set we see a man studying at his desk and he is killed by a gangster. This scene is repeated two more times and each time the victim and the killer change their roles. This scene also implies the idea of ambiguity, chance and possibility. The mother and the daughter see the three versions of the murder and following this scene there appears a soloist who is a variant of the mother and she starts singing the Beckett libretto. As one scene follows the other, we see many more variants of the mother and daughter couple. We see mothers and daughters of different ages. Just in the case of alive and dead cats we see the mothers and daughters alive and dead, animate and inanimate and robot and human. Additionally, we see groups of gangsters, miners and police officers.

Even with this brief description of the play we have the basic ideas related to the structure of the play. There is not the unfolding of a well-made story with a beginning, middle and ending and there are no traditional characters. We do not have a story line and no characters but only shadows and free-floating images. We watch the parade of images, figures and transforming beings along with animals on stage. Upon describing the stage and setting the ground for the discussion, we can move on to commenting on the details. First, we can start with the mother and daughter figures. As we have mentioned above, the figures appear in different scenes throughout the play and the daughter is replaced with a robot in the following scenes and we see the robot exhaling smoke and then we see the dead body of the daughter which has been autopsied by a group of doctors. The doctors cover the body of the girl and hand it to another group on stage. The body of the daughter changes from animate to inanimate and from organic body to a robot. Likewise, the mother changes throughout the scenes. First, she wears a mask with a frozen facial expression and then her body is replaced with the body of a mannequin. We watch the passage of her body from animate to inanimate. With the bodies of the two main figures we have the animals and machines. The cat reenters the stage on several occasions throughout the play and then we also see a dog then a horse dancing amid the fog clouds. The machines also have an important place in the unfolding scenes. We see a car and a train. The train has the power to destroy the unity of the bodies on stage. It comes increasingly closer to the body of the mother and it runs over the mother and the mother loses her leg after this accident. Thereafter the leg which is set free from the body stands in front of a microphone and stays silently. Somehow, it is the silent scream of the body whose unity has been destroyed.

Let me put it sketchily to be able to go further, I can say that we have the bodies replaced by robots and mannequins and we have the animals occupying the stage center and the machines destroying the bodily unity of the figures. Now, we can start commenting on the main point around which we can gather all the implications we have drawn so far. As we have stated in the very beginning of the discussion, the absence is the basic strategy that Romeo Castellucci has adopted. We cannot see a story line and traditional characters. The first step in this journey has been taken by Gertrude Stein and Samuel Beckett. Taking all these discussions and groundbreaking practices at hand Heiner Goebbels has set the absence as an aesthetic strategy. All these strategies have been used by Romeo Castellucci. For this reason, I can say that his research and practices can be seen within the frame of posthumanism addressing all previous implications.

In *Neither*, the unity of the body is either destroyed or the bodies are replaced by inanimate bodies. I intend to use this as the meeting point and I would like to take my discussion one step further. To be able achieve this we can go back to Rosi Braidotti one more time. She develops her argument by setting the ground of humanism as the underlying idea behind western thinking. The humanist way of seeing the world has its roots in art, philosophy and culture. According to Rosi Braidotti humanism has an equal meaning with civilization in the Western world. In that sense she pronounces a kind of anti-humanistic point of view in her discussion. And she crafts a posthumanist challenge:

> In other words, the posthumanist position I am defending builds on the anti-humanist legacy, more specifically on the epistemological and political foundations of the poststructuralist generation and moves further. The alternative views about the human and the new formations of subjectivity that have emerged from the radical epistemologies of Continental philosophy in the last thirty years do not merely oppose Humanism but create other visions of the self. Sexualized, racialized and naturalized differences, far from being the categorical boundary-keepers of the subject of Humanism, have evolved into fully fledged alternative models of the human subject.[4]

---

4   Rosi Braidotti, The Posthuman, Cambridge, Polity Press, 2013, p.38.

The "the posthumanist position" Rosi Braidotti uses in her discussion opens a prolific and vast ground before us on which I can settle and develop my ideas. She claims that this position has an anti-humanist background and it has a close link with poststructuralist approaches. The terms and ideas that I have gathered up to this point have also strong connections with poststructuralist ideas. Stein, Beckett and Goebbels and their theories and practices can all be perceived within this structural frame and their legacy, especially Gertrude Stein's, sets the foundations on which Castellucci builds his version of *Neither*. Taking all these ideas into consideration and putting Castellucci's overall practices under the magnifying glass I feel entitled to comment on the play. It is the right time to talk about "alternative views about human" as we are following the shades in the play. The human loses his central presence and goes to the edge where he meets the mannequin, the animal, the robot. To be able to talk about the new beings on stage we inevitably need "new formations of subjectivity". The godlike presence of the author has disappeared, and we cannot talk about any kind of character but beings. The boundaries became blurred between human/animal, animate/inanimate and organic/material. The members of the audience feel the power to build new relations between the new subjects on stage. The subjects have no objects to create a hierarchy with and that's why the subject/object beings stand still and call for new meanings in the eyes of the spectators. Rosi Braidotti explains this inter-connection:

> An altogether different and powerful source of inspiration for contemporary re-configurations of critical posthumanism is ecology and environmentalism. They rest on an enlarged sense of inter-connection between self and others, including the non-human or 'earth' others. This practice of relating to others requires and is enhanced by the rejection of self-centered individualism. It produces a new way of combining self-interests with the well-being of an enlarged community, based on environmental inter-connections.[5]

In this sense the inter-connection goes beyond the blurred borders of human/animal and reaches out to other kinds of relation between the beings on earth, which reminds us of Gertrude Stein's definition of landscape in which each detail is linked to the other details. And the idea of

---

5   Rosi Braidotti, The Posthuman, Cambridge, Polity Press, 2013, pp. 47–48.

inter-connectedness can bring the idea of "healing the Earth and that which has been so cruelly disconnected."[6] The idea of abolishing the borders and of blurring the lines between human beings, animals and materials gives us the opportunity of a more holistic approach towards a new conception of the subject and this takes through an ending which is not an end actually.

And this paper is nothing but a first attempt to conceptualize the idea of posthumanism in performing arts and it employs some preliminary terms to comment on the new aesthetic approach in this field by rethinking the earliest examples in theater and trying to combine them with the recent ideas in philosophy. Posthumanism is a rather new term and can be said to setting a slippery ground to talk about performing arts. Beginning in the first decades of 20th century and through the 1950s, theatre lost its supposedly fixed grounding on "unities", opening up new possibilities. Heiner Goebbels can be seen among the most important key figures who created a bridge between the first and second halves of the 20th century and upon whose aesthetic understanding we can build many new ideas of the posthumanist stage. As a researcher trying to find my way through the displaced paths, I intend to start a new discussion around those ideas yet I always feel the need to take my steps cautiously during this journey as the disembodied beings travel with me and they continuously challenge my ideas. Nonetheless, I always take delight in walking among these shadows and struggle hard to touch them on a new aesthetic scape. The German playwright and director Heiner Müller once said in an interview with film-maker Alexander Kluge: "[w]hat occupies the space, can change all the time. It does not have to be human being, it can also be a computer or an herbal substance, whatever."[7] In front of us there lies a vast and uncanny scape and the images can move like the trees in Birnam Wood in *Macbeth*.

6   Rosi Braidotti, The Posthuman, Cambridge, Polity Press, 2013, p.48.
7   Quoted from Heiner Müller by Kristof van Baarle, The Routledge Companion to Theatre and Politics, New York, Routledge, 2019, p.228.

Özlem Karadağ

Ecofeminist Ecopoetics and Carol Ann Duffy

Carol Ann Duffy, who brought together "poems about our vanishing insect world" for *The Guardian* (2019), has claimed that "When we demean language, we demean our lives, our society and ultimately our planet. Poetry stands against this, timelessly, in Sappho, Shakespeare, John Donne, Emily Dickinson" ("Into thin air"). During a time when Brexit heavily overshadowed Britain, Duffy considers environmental poems are more crucial than the political ones, because the ecological crisis is more urgent and affected directly by human actions. Duffy, who served as the first female poet laureate of the United Kingdom between 2009 and 2019, is a poet who thinks that everything on this Earth is connected, and she believes that poets are primarily responsible towards this planet. Although Duffy does not refer to herself as an ecofeminist poet or to her poetry as environmental, her approach to nature and generally subjugated human and nonhuman other(s) positions her poetry as ecofeminist ecopoetics, two approaches that are united in this context to read Carol Ann Duffy's poetry.

Duffy's poems reveal a desire to pay homage to those who are oppressed and silenced by the patriarchal order, which is a white-Western-male-oriented system that is biased against mostly people of color, women, nonhuman animals,[1] and nature with a misplaced concept of humanism. Furthermore, the main characteristic of her poetry is the way she uses language. She reloads words with new meanings and aims at uniting each life form on the planet, from humans to nonhuman animals through the use of this language. She also brings a critical approach to the way we use language to label, discriminate and even distance ourselves from the

---

1   In *Zoopoetics: Animals and the Making of Poetry*, Aaron M. Moe suggests that "Phrases such as 'nonhuman animals' [...] still marks animals by something they are not. They are not human" (x). Although I find his argument understandable I prefer using human and nonhuman animals without the intention of underlining the idea that animals are not human.

harm we inflict on nature. As Duffy refrains from putting labels or creating new oppositions in her approach to marginalized entities, her poems give hope for the future of understanding and redefining our relationship with language and our planet.

Ecofeminism advocates an understanding of human and nonhuman animals as equal beings in nature and also tries to create a planet in which nature and all species live equally in all their complexities, avoiding definitions, labels and discrimination of any kind.[2] Ecopoetics, tries to achieve this by changing the position of nature and nonhuman animals in poetry with a particular concern for environmental problems created by the anthropocentric world view. Jonathan Skinner, the editor of *ecopoetics*, introduces the term in the first issue of the journal as follows:

> *ecopoetics* nevertheless takes on the "eco" frame, in recognition that human impact on the Earth and its other species, is without a doubt the historical watershed of our generation, a generation born in the second half of the twentieth century. [...]
> "Eco" here signals—no more, no less—the house we share with several million other species, our planet Earth. "Poetics" is used as poesis or making, not necessarily to emphasize the critical over the creative act (nor vice versa). Thus: ecopoetics, a house making. (7)

Accordingly, ecopoetics, deriving from the Greek word -*oikos* (as in ecology) meaning home, is not just an attempt of house-making with the use of an untraditional device as poetics, it is also very much connected to the idea of nature as our home with an endeavor to understand and redefine human position in it through poetry.

Green poetry, as Terry Gifford puts it (*Green Voices* 3), can be considered as a general term that refers to all types of nature poetry; however, it is crucial to see how ecopoetics stands apart from the others. Traditional nature

---

2 Except for the non-environmentalist "cornucopian position" that reveres nature "only [...] in terms of its usefulness" (Garrard 18) to humanity, each significant position in environmentalism recognises the source of the crisis as anthropocentrism. However, they fall short in recognizing it as androcentrism, therefore ecofeminism, as an embodiment of diversity and pluralism, suggests that the solutions presented by the others fail to cover the environmental crisis to the fullest (See Birkeland).

poetry, classical or Romantic pastoral,[3] and ecopoetry, all these subgenres of green poetry focus on a different way of human interaction with nature, yet, ecopoetics differs from these in its approach. Environmental concerns or concerns about human use and abuse of nature and nonhuman animals, and the question of putting these issues on the page are at the core of ecopoetics. Sarah Nolan puts forward what underlies ecopoetry and ecopoetics in her book *Unnatural Ecopoetics: Unlikely Spaces in Contemporary Poetry*:

> Pointing to popular environmental literary and social trends, many scholars and poets view ecopoetics and ecopoetry as involved in politicized movements to make poetry relevant to current real-world concerns, often without much or any recognition of the theory behind the term "ecopoetics." [...] "ecopoetry" has come to refer to poetry that engages with environments for the sake of political and social action, while "ecopoetics" is a methodology or theoretical lens that considers the nuances of how environmental experiences are expressed on the page. [...] Regardless of the variations in its definition, ecopoetics generally tends to involve analyzing how poems move beyond idealized interactions with the physical world and begin to represent nature for its own inherent value and autonomous self. (Introduction)

Moving from this definition of ecopoetics, which differentiates the term from other types of poetry that focus on nature, it can be suggested that since the last decades of the 20th century and of course with the threatening effects of ecological crisis, this ecological turn in theory and poetry finds its full voice, it differs not only in its approach to nature, human, and nonhuman animals but also in its use of language, it aims to deconstruct the mainstream ideology with an attempt to show the possibility of change

---

3   The word pastoral derives from "pastorem (pastor), Latin for shepherd" (Hoad 339) and as a genre came into being in the Hellenistic period, it is dominantly nostalgic as human beings are already cut off from nature. According to this viewpoint, in classical pastoral, it is possible to see how nature is crushed by civilisation and left out of the city's boundaries. It can also be suggested that pastoral romanticizes the cultivated version of nature as the word itself derives from an agricultural human society. Therefore, Romantic pastoral (and the desire to return to nature as a reaction to the Industrial Revolution) is also based upon the desire to go back to a tamed version of nature. Thus, with nature poetry, in the traditional sense, comes the androcentric outlook on nature, as these literary traditions are mostly male-dominated.

through the construction of a completely new discourse and approach.[4] This new approach can be seen as the birth of ecofeminist ecopoetics, a term that brings together the environmental considerations of both ideas and Carol Ann Duffy can be read as one of the most important representatives of this approach.

As a prolific poet actively writing since the late 20th century, Duffy is often seen as a descendant of the male poets of the recent past such as Philip Larkin. In reply to this comparison with Larkin, Duffy states that: "Poetry has changed since the days of Larkin – he's a good poet, but poetry has changed for the better. It's not a bunch of similarly educated men – it's many voices, many styles. The edge has become the centre" (Winterson, "Can you move diagonally"). This quotation can be a proof of not only the change in poetry, but it also marks the changes in Duffy's poetry, which becomes, as Peter Forbes coins it, "Duffyesque" ("Winning lines"). Jeanette Winterson in her article "Rereading Carol Ann Duffy" explores Duffy's *The World's Wife* and claims that the collection is "of course [...] political" and she adds that "Duffy's 1999 collection [...] gives the women behind the scenes [...] a glorious and powerful voice". As Winterson comments upon the women in her poetry, Duffyesque does not appear just for the sake of supporting an ideology, it stands as the poet's way of understanding the world and the change she wants to create with this powerful literary tool. As Dowson suggests "when Duffy sings the earth, she takes account of the 'complex web of nature and environment' (Bate 2000: 23)" (170). Her topics, speakers, choice of places vary from cities to wild nature, nonhuman animals to spirits of literary or mythological characters and her poems centralize the marginalized others, explore human beings in relation to other human beings, animals, and their habitat, which mostly reveal the hypocrisy of the dominant patriarchal humanism.

---

4   Even in the twentieth and twenty-first centuries, so many critical texts on ecology and nature poetry are written mostly by men, and they mostly focus on the poems written by male poets which still fall short in terms of ecofeminist criticism. These attempts can be considered as a part of "manstream green theories" and as Birkeland suggests "Manstream green theories are gender-blind, they do not adequately challenge the underlying bases of the ethic and ideology that they seek to change" (26).

In "Model Village" (*Selling Manhattan),* maybe also as a result of tech-nological and scientific "advancements" in agriculture that drastically affected nature, Duffy creates a mock-pastoral. It can also be read as anti-pastoral or post-pastoral as Terry Gifford coins the terms (*Green Voices),* because she brings a critical approach to the idea of pastoral bliss of a rural town. She describes the town through a child's words, a place where "Cows say *Moo*" and "Sheep say *Baa.* Grass is green" (79), on the sur-face what looks like a picture-perfect village with its farm animals and child-like innocence, with the words and stanzas in italics that reveal the inner thoughts of the villagers and the anthropocentric language turn into a dark image of the Anthropocene. It starts as "a picture-book depiction of a rural English community and, as it were, draws back the net curtains to reveal a sick state of affairs" (Dowson 118). The speaker's words reveal the androcentric mindset that the child will grow into, a world that normalizes the utilitarian approach: "Hens say *Cluck* and give us eggs. Pigs/are pink and give us sausages. *Grunt,* they say" (79). The sounds animals make are in italics all through the poem, and it underlines the idea that these are human intonations of animal sounds which remove them from their original selves and make them farm animals. The same lines also show the normalization of farm animals' duties toward humans such as giving eggs and in pigs' case giving sausages, and they are not recognized for any other form of existence other than their human-made responsibilities. Karen J. Warren explains the importance of language as follows:

> Many philosophers (e.g., Ludwig Wittgenstein) have argued that the language one uses mirrors and reflects one's concept of oneself and one's world. As such, language plays a crucial role in concept formation. Ecofeminists argue that it also plays a crucial role in keeping intact mutually reinforcing sexist, racist, and naturist views of women, people of color, and nonhuman nature. (27)

Parallel to the ecofeminist view of language, Duffy achieves to show how the seemingly innocent language of the child is not innocent at all, as it reflects the androcentric view of nonhuman animals and nature, and completely controls the formation of the child's mind. Moreover, the lines "The Grocer has a parrot. Parrots say *Pretty Polly/*and *Who's a pretty boy then*" (81) not only come as a reminder of colonization of distant lands and imperialism but also as a symbol that shows how others, non-human animals and indigenous people, were torn apart from their natural environments and forced to become completely different beings in a British background. That is why the speaker, the child, is not able to learn the real sounds a parrot makes but thinks that these human sentences are the sounds all parrots make. As the villagers also dream of other possibilities, Miss Maiden poisons her mother, the farmer is *"Digging, desperately"* (80), the vicar *"can feel the naughtiness under* [his] *smock"* (80), and for the librarian "Outside is chaos,/lives with no sense of plot" (81), and they are all afraid of one another, "The Vicar is nervous/of parrots, isn't he? Miss Maiden is nervous of Vicar and the Farmer is nervous of everything" (81). This seemingly blissful and perfect image of the village, therefore pastoral in general, are not representing the truth about the anthropocentric domination of nature as this model village does.

What is also criticized here is the fact that nature, and its organic ties with all the species and inanimate things in it, is reduced to Anthropocene. The same criticism can be seen in Duffy's exploration of anthropocentrism's effects on nature in the city, as well. In "The English Elms" (*The Bees*) she offers a critical view of how the city devours nature,[5] as the poem talks about the historical roots of "Seven Sisters in Tottenham" in north London. Seven Sisters were English elms that used to be in Tottenham which are "long gone, except for their names" (467). The speaker of the poem continues with the following lines:

> Others stood at the edge of farms,
> twinned with the shapes of clouds
> like green rhymes;
> or cupped the beads of rain
> in their leaf palms;
> or glowered, grim giants, warning storms. (467)

---

5   The earliest example of man and civilization taking over nature can be found in the first lines of *the Epic of Gilgamesh*, one of the earliest examples of epic poetry. In the poem, the poet-persona introduces Gilgamesh as a great king mostly for building the "rampart of Uruk-the-Sheepfold" (1.11) as a means of urbanisation and cutting bonds with nature. Gilgamesh, stops bullying his people and directs his attention to Humbaba, the guardian of the sacred Cedar Forest, so nature becomes his main enemy: After killing and cutting the head of Humbaba, the first thing they do is to find the tallest tree in the forest and cut it down to build a door in the city for Enlil (46–47).

These lines reveal a fact about the past days of London as a city that not only had farms and trees that conveyed the language of nature, but also a city that did not have the present cityscape until the recent past. As the poem also mentions, it is possible to see them "In the hedgerows in old films", and it is an elegy for the loss of these trees which can only be found "in the lines of poems […] for ours is a world without them" (467). Although the poem's main subjects are the English elms, the general tone is one that mourns for the loss of the trees and the life form that is associated with them. Maria Mies in "White Man's Dilemma: His Search for, What He Has Destroyed" indicates that this kind of destruction brings with it a desire to escape to not-yet-urbanised places to enjoy nature:

> In the urban centres of the industrialised North may be observed a curious mass behaviour from time to time. Those who apparently consider urban culture and lifestyle as the pinnacle of progress and modernity for whom the cities are centres of 'Life', of freedom, of culture, rush away from these very cities whenever they can. A flight into 'Nature', the 'wilderness', 'underdeveloped' countries of the South, to areas where White Man, they hope, has not yet 'penetrated'. (132)

Unfortunately, this destructive pattern spreads to these places that are considered to be natural yet underdeveloped, which leads to the urbanization of relatively "untouched" parts of nature. Henri Lefebvre, in *Writings on Cities*, suggests that "[A] theme which has been used and over-used, hyperinflated and extrapolated, namely, 'nature and culture', originates from the relation between town and country and deflects it" (118) and he underlines the "sacred-damned character of the ground" (118) which is used by cities to change and abuse its position as desired. However, he also suggests that in our age "urban life penetrates peasant life, dispossessing it of its traditional features" (119) which will eventually lead to "the urban […] to disappear" (120) as urbanity is taking over nature, it also erases the opposition that creates or defines what is urban. For all the lands inhabited by human beings that represent the dominant culture turn into a big city out of concrete, and as Duffy puts in her poem these long-gone trees appear in literature and art, therefore, in our age, language and literature become essential tools to keep nature alive. Dowson scrutinises that "Duffy is neither a 'city' nor a 'post-industrial' poet for her engagement with urban life is not at odds with her self-fashioned task of championing aspects of culture threatened by human insouciance and these include nature" (166).

Duffyesque ecofeminist ecopoetics can critically contemplate on the relationship between nature and its inhabitants by revealing different forms of
endangered lives by the Anthropocene.

Nonhuman animals are recurrent subjects of her poetry, and in each
of her poems, she is able to recreate this subject divergently. The recurrent image of nonhuman animals in her poems can also be considered as
zoopoetics, Derrida coins the term in his work *The Animal That Therefore
I Am*, and zoopoetics "generally refer[s] to the presence of animals within
any genre" (Moe 11). In "The Dolphins" (*Standing Female Nude*) Duffy
explores animal cruelty through choosing her poet persona as a dolphin
trapped in an aqua park. The dolphin who talks to the audience saying
"We see our silver skin flash by like memory/of somewhere else" (59)
goes beyond the Aristotelian or Cartesian characteristics of animals, as
the former suggests only human beings have the capability of recalling
memories at will (Aristotle 6) and the latter claims that the human beings
are different from animals due to free will, reason, and soul (Descartes
14-16). These abilities can also be read as anthropomorphism as an animal
is given capabilities associated with humans such as guilt, translating, and
loving; however, Duffy is not following the androcentric pattern, she gives
these capacities to the dolphin under a very natural tone even by paying
careful attention not to name or attribute gender to the dolphins through
the mouth of the speaker. The speaker refers to the other dolphin sharing
the pool only as "the other" with whom it shows an inevitable close connection yet the general atmosphere is a depressive one as the dolphins are
stuck in a pool and forced by a man to jump the hoops and play with a
plastic ball until he disappears. The only thing defined by its sex in the
poem is the man, who represents humanity in general but of course dominantly the domineering power of masculinity which can be defined as
androcentrism through an ecofeminist point of view.

As a matter of fact, in the poem, Duffy carefully avoids using gender
pronouns or possessives, and the dolphin, the speaker of the poem, refers
to the other dolphin as "the other" but without its traditional discrimi-
nating meaning, without the speaker's superiority over the other. It also
enables the dolphin to speak about the other dolphin without any prejudiced or judgmental adjectives. The only one in the poem whose gender
we know is the man, so the perpetrator is clearly defined as a male and as

Dowson suggests it can be anyone who is oppressed and victimized by this man, who symbolises an ideological standing.

In every poem she talks about nonhuman animals and nature, although her speakers use familiar words and sentence structures in English, Duffy pays special attention to the way they define or describe the way they each understand other languages and their environment through different parts and characteristics of their bodies. The two dolphins try to translate the language of the water of the pool through their flesh yet they fail: "We have found no truth in these waters,/no explanations tremble on our flesh" (59). Because the still waters of the pool, which is their human-made prison, is dead to them, it is a language they cannot fully comprehend. As Dowson suggests "the water signifies learned language in which the dolphins are captive – 'we have found no truth in these waters' – and in which they lose their being – 'our mind knows we will die here'" (33) whereas the very first line of the poem is ambivalent in meaning: "World is what you swim in, or dance, it is simple." This line can be read as the definition of the world for the dolphins yet as it is followed by "We are in our element but we are not free./Outside this world you cannot breathe for long" which suddenly turn this world upside down and squeeze it into the limits of the pool, the water in it is their "element", but they are not "free".

They are captivated by the man, the only thing they recognize besides the hoop and the plastic ball. The connection created between the three and what they degrade the dolphins to are presented to the reader through the language used by a dolphin which symbolises all captivated animals and all mammals, as Dowson indicates "it is through language that Duffy expresses the mammals' captivity, also a metaphor for any group or individual that feels confined: 'There is a man/and there are hoops.' In this simple sentence, Duffy makes familiar objects, 'man' and 'hoops', seem strange, almost sinister. Yet, it is with this sense of something 'unreal' that we identify" (33). Duffy achieves to make this ordinary, androcentric language sound completely different through her speaker which turns into zoopoetics, as Moe suggests "zoopoetics focuses on the process by which animals are makers. They make texts. They gesture. They vocalise. The sounds and vocalisations emerge from a rhetorical body, a poetic body, or rather a body that is able *to make*" (11). The Dolphin, as the speaker, lets the reader imagine the creation of this text disregarding the fact that it is a poem written in English. What becomes more important is the way the dolphin constructs this language which becomes a form of zoopoetics.

John Berger in "Why Look at Animals?" discusses that a zoo is another "public institution" founded in the late eighteenth, early nineteenth century, and "public zoos were an endorsement of the modern colonial power. The capturing of the animals was a symbolic representation of the conquest of all distant and exotic lands" (21). It can be suggested that in our postcolonial world animals are still commodities to be colonized and consumed, for not only zoos but also entertainment business such as circuses or aqua parks still exist to put nonhuman animals on display to be viewed by human beings. Moreover, Berger also suggests that these animals are "collected in order that they can be seen, observed, studied. [...] Yet in the zoo the view is always wrong" (23), the popular image inscribed in our minds concerning dolphins is the one where dolphins are thought to smile and be a true friend to human beings,[6] also having fun entertaining people, yet this is the way human beings see it through a distorted spectacle, forgetting the truth behind animal abuse. Therefore, Duffy turns the marginalised dolphins into central figures who voice their truth and also reveal that they are not only seen, but they also see and are very much aware that they are seen, but this fact is also completely disregarded by human beings. Derrida in *The Animal That Therefore I Am* talks about the gaze of the animal as follows: "[A]s with every bottomless gaze, as with the eyes of the other, the gaze called 'animal' offers [...] the abyssal limit of the human: the inhuman or the ahuman, the ends of man" (12). Moving from this idea, one can suggest that human beings who are blinded by the androcentric outlook, also to feel better about their actions, choose to consider nonhuman animals as beings without the capacity of seeing, understanding, and judging.

The subject of nonhuman animals can also be traced in "A Healthy Meal" (*Standing Female Nude*) in which Duffy introduces the reader to

---

6   With the twentieth-century, movies and TV-series such as *Flipper* (1963, 1964, 1964–67, 1995–2000), *Lassie* (1954–74), *Skipper* (1968–77), *Jaws* (1975, 1978, 1987) and many others not only attribute certain anthropomorphic characteristics to animals but also instil these prejudiced and mostly wrong ideas concerning animals in our collective memory.

the hypocrisy of meat-eating humans. As a poem that supports vegetarianism, it shows the anthropocentric hypocritical attitude towards nonhuman animals as well as a fake feeling of guilt that is easily disregarded with the use of language. Mentioning of "oxtail" on an "earthen dish", "wishbones and pinkies", "a kidney or the breast of something which once flew", "tongues [...] Leg, saddle and breast" (61) and the like being served as dishes on a table or a menu deliberately put together to show human beings' use and abuse of every part of nonhuman animals. As Duffy puts it "The menu lists the recent dead" (61), for the murdered animals are displayed on the menu under different names that detach them from their past as living beings and turn them into dishes. "Fingerbowls", traditionally served at the end of dinner, and "napkins" are ironically mentioned because they show how easy it is for people to wash away their fake guilt. In *The Sexual Politics of Meat*, Carol J. Adams suggests that "Animals are made absent through language that renames dead bodies before consumers participate in eating them. Our culture further mystifies the term 'meat' with gastronomic language, so we do not conjure dead, butchered animals, but cuisine. Language thus contributes even further to animals' absences" (2010, 66). Duffy criticizes the use of language to diminish the effect of meat-eating, which is more about killing an animal and washing away the guilt, as she says in the poem "Alter *calf* to *veal* in four attempts. This is/the power of words; knife, tripe, lights, charcuterie" (61). The four attempts not only stand for the process from knife to charcuterie but also for the four letters that come together and change a calf into a veal, that is why she chooses to write these words in italics.

In the poem, Duffy specifies two human beings describing one as "a fat man" who "orders his *rare* and a fine sweat/bastes his face" and the other as "the woman chewing suckling pig" (61) which prove that it is not specific to a gender. However, it is more about taking part in androcentric ideology regardless of one's gender. Janis Birkeland in her attempt to define ecofeminist theory distinguishes two contrasting "orientations" as "masculinist" and "feminist," clarifying that she uses the terms "as metaphorical icons for systems of value to which people of either sex can subscribe" (15) with a desire to show that the problem is about the mindset rather than sex. Hence, as Birkeland suggests, the poem is not trying to falsely single out and accuse a group of people depending on their gender but blames the hypocritical attitude of any man or woman who shares this androcentric attitude that victimizes nonhuman animals. It can be said that human beings still use old ideas concerning nonhuman animals believing in the duality of body and soul. Along with Descartes, who sees animals as machines created by nature which "absolves [men] from the suspicion of crime when they eat or kill animals" (19), humanity still embraces Immanuel Kant's approach to animals as "man's instruments", who abstains cruelty to animals only because "our duties towards animals are merely indirect duties towards humanity" (240). However, ecofeminists "reject the nature/culture dualism of patriarchal thought, and locate animals and humans within nature" (Gaard, "Living Interconnections" 6) and Duffy attempts to show how the language is a patriarchal construction and how it moves us away from the reality of animal cruelty and the guilt that should surround it.

Her approach makes it possible to read her poetry through vegetarian ecofeminist outlook for "Vegetarian ecofeminists argue that only by forestalling our sympathies for other animals are humans able to overlook the enormity of animal suffering" (Gaard, "Vegetarian Ecofeminism" 119). As can be seen in "Model Village", Duffy underlines the fact that our ties with nature and nonhuman animals are cut very early, in Lacanian terms, with our entrance into the Symbolic Order, hence it gets more difficult for human beings to sympathise or empathise with the pain of the others. Warren suggests that "the view of humans, like their nonhuman animal kin, as both eater and eaten is an *ecological* view that puts humans where they belong ecologically – as part of nature and part of the food chain. This is the ecological piece sorely missing from animal welfarist accounts of humans" (136) nevertheless this view imagines human beings harmoniously living in nature and not seeing animals, or the others in general, as meat. Whereas the situation for the Western, or Westernized, industrial societies is entirely the opposite, therefore, in Warren's words again "Ecofeminist animal rights welfarists [...] argue that factory farming, animal experimentation, hunting, and meat-eating are tied to patriarchal concepts and practices" (Warren 25).

The word "rare" in the above quotation from the poem is also written in italics by the poet to stress the idea of eating (raw) meat and the thin line between cannibalism and meat-eating. Cannibalism, which is seen as barbaric and uncultivated by the civilized Western point of view, was and still is an established fear of "regression into barbarism" (Huggan & Tiffin 63), is overlooked when meat-eating is a part of a gourmet experience. Berger indicates that "[A] peasant becomes fond of his pig and is glad to salt away its pork. What is significant, and is so difficult for the urban stranger to understand, is that the two statements in that sentence are connected by an *and* not by a *but*" (7). However, what is easy for the urban dweller in our modern age is not having any kind of bonds with the animal when they are eating meat. As Duffy criticizes, the problem is more about disregarding the ugly truth behind meat-eating in our civilized, industrialized societies, as we disregard animal cruelty by hiding behind Cartesian or Kantian pragmatism in our approach to nonhuman animals. That is why the poem ends with the line "Death moves in the bowels. You are what you eat" (61), and Duffy, of course, connects civilized societies with murder and cannibalism; and not only in terms of meat-eating practices but more on a general note, as it entails feeding upon and harming nonhuman animals and natural resources through different ways of colonization.

Warren suggests that for ecofeminists "trees, water, food production, animals, toxins, and, more generally, naturism (i.e. the unjustified domination of nonhuman nature) are feminist issues" and comprehending naturism is vital because it "helps one understand the interconnections among the dominations of women and other subordinated groups of humans [...] and the domination of nonhuman nature" (Warren 1–2). Duffy's poetry attempts to come to an understanding of these "interconnections", in "Selling Manhattan" (*Selling Manhattan*) she tries to show not only the opposition created by colonial forces but also the close connections between people of color, women, nonhuman others and nature in Native America. For her poems in *Selling Manhattan*, Duffy suggests that "*Selling Manhattan* is mainly about loss. The poems explore the loss of contact with true values, and there's an ecological theme that ties in with that [...] I suppose I'm trying to shape through language things which are outside of it; to give a voice to those whom we've denied a voice, attempts at pre-language" (quoted in Dowson 9). In "Selling Manhattan", with the innovative use of language and styling, she represents not only how the white Western patriarchal domination colonizes and penetrates, pollutes,

and abuses everything that is considered as the other, but also gives voice
to the mind and the mindset of the colonized, dominated marginals, and
their loss.

Dowson recounts that the poem is woven around historical facts
concerning exploitation as it "re-enacts the historical myth that Dutch
explorers exploited Native Americans by purchasing the island for $24
worth of beads and trinkets. There is evidence of this in the Dutch archives
although contemporary commentators argue that the 60 gilders paid for
New York's Manhattan Island were worth more like one thousand dollars
in 1626" (Dowson 95). Contemporary commentators' argument is another
point open to discussion as it may easily be criticized in terms of ethics;
however, the main criticism in the poem surrounds not only economic
exploitation but the exploitation of a nature-dominant culture. The poem
starts with the colonizer's lines written in italics and reveals the mindset
of the white Western-patriarchal ideology of the discriminative and utilitarian colonizer:

> All yours, Injun, twenty-four bucks' worth of glass beads,
> gaudy cloth. I got myself a bargain. I brandish
> fire-arms and fire-water. Praise the Lord.
> Now get your red ass out of here. (94)

Starting with the offensive word Injun, Duffy places the Western colonizer into a position that he claims superiority and dominance over the
marginalised other.

There is not only a great divide between the colonizer and the colonized in terms of the language they use, but also in the way they use it.
Their approach to humanity and nature in general also differs drastically.
The colonizer represents violence and militarism as he brandishes his
"fire-arms", his language is dominated by verbal violence, and he takes
all this power from the Lord he praises, the Christian God that, gave the
white-Western-Christian men the power over all others. As Lynn White
Jr suggests, the beginning of our ecological crisis can be traced back to
the birth of Christianity, because "Christianity, in absolute contrast to
ancient paganism [...], not only established a dualism of man and nature
but also insisted that it is God's will that man exploit nature for his proper
ends" and "By destroying pagan animism, Christianity made it possible to
exploit nature in a mood of indifference to the feelings of natural objects"

(10). Only in four lines in italics, and through her general use of italics in her poetry, Duffy lets the ugly truth about the white-Western-Christian androcentric ideologies reveal itself. In this poem, italics also become a set of language that signifies the discourse of the exploiters.

In contrast, the discourse she creates for the colonized-other completely contrasts the colonizer's, so using the same language but by changing not only the style but also the word choices she is able to show the power of language and how it can be constructed and used in a completely different way: "The brutally superior yet vulgar voice of the Christian coloniser who praises the Lord but plays god (…) contrasts to the pantheistic spirituality of the gentle man he boots out [...] Thus, Duffy gives the high poetic lines to this unmaterialistic native" (Dowson 96). Although Dowson, recognizes the speaker of the poem as a male, Duffy refrains from assigning a specific gender to her speaker. She also tries to refrain from using any gendered pronouns when referring to humans, nonhuman animals and nature, except for the line when the "native" speaker of the poem calls out to the colonizer saying: "Man who fears death, how many acres do you need/to lengthen your shadow under the endless sky" (94). It can be suggested that this colonizer is no different than the man the dolphin mentions in "The Dolphins", as they both exploit and harm nature. Nevertheless, this use of language without gender-specific nouns and pronouns, and any negative anthropomorphic or theriomorphic representations are dominant to Duffy's poetry. It is parallel to ecofeminist ideas concerning language, according to Warren "Euro-American language is riddled with examples of 'sexist-naturist language,' that is, language that depicts women, animals, and nonhuman nature as inferior to (having less status, value, or prestige than) men and male-identified culture" (27). Duffy, although she uses one of the Euro-American languages, achieves to use it in so many different forms that she proves the possibility of shaping a language that can be divorced from all its discriminative and dominative characteristics.

The same line also points out to a difference in the colonizer's and the colonized one's approach to life and death. While the colonizer is materialistic, utilitarian and self-confident about his reason and power over the world, he is still afraid of death and disrespectful to nature. In contrast, the speaker of the poem is not afraid of death and believes in the continuation of life through reincarnation or merging of different life forms. The speaker says "I will live in the ghost of grasshopper and buffalo" (95), and rather than seeing it as degrading as Western civilization does, respects and loves the course nature takes "I sing with true love for the land;/dawn chant, the song sunset, starlight psalm" and also reveals that each element of nature is a lesson: "I have learned/the solemn laws of joy and sorrow, in the distance/between morning's frost and firefly's flash at night" (94). On the contrary, the colonizer continues harming nature; the speaker says "Wherever/you have touched the earth, the earth is sore" (94) which is most probably a reference to the penetrating and harmful behavior of the capitalist-colonizer cultures through eco-unfriendly agriculture, mining, deforestation and domination.

The speaker, who is amazed to see that the colonizer aims to own "the rivers and the grass", shows how the outlook of the colonized one is different from the domineering and destructive aims of the white-Western-patriarchal culture. A culture that always ends in harming nature, as the poem also suggests, *he* will "poison it", "freedom" will "vanish" and there will be "silence" (94) following this loss which is a reference to the sounds of nature and other languages. What Duffy tries to do in this poem is to go back in history, to a time before the coming of silence (silencing through colonization/civilization), and record the song and the words of a not-yet-colonized America.

The speaker in "Selling Manhattan" can be a female or a male, but most importantly exists beyond the gendered structure of the Western World. If we are to consider the speaker as a female, and take into consideration the bond ecofeminists see between nature and woman, "Wherever/you have touched the earth, the earth is sore" (94) can also be read as the rape of the body and the land because "Some ecofeminists connect violence against women through rape [...] to violence against nature" (Warren 25) and vice versa. However, Duffy refrains from such a clear connection and creates an all-inclusive, all-embracing connectedness in nature. Thus, Duffy's careful attempt to create a poetic language that does not use gender and possessive nouns or pronouns, except for a number of men who are the perpetrators of nature's destruction, is in accordance with ecofeminism. For Warren "language that feminises nature *in a patriarchal culture*, where women are viewed as subordinate and inferior, reinforces and authorises the domination of nature. The Mother Nature (not Father Nature) is raped, mastered, controlled, conquered, mined" (Warren 27). Even when her speakers are women as in "Thetis" (*The World's Wife*), in which she rewrites the story of a Greek goddess that is associated with nature but known only because of her son Achilles, Duffy is concerned about making women's unheard stories more prominent. She aims to reveal not only the way they are one with all beings but also how they are taken for granted, abused, and even destroyed by the androcentric outlook.

Although *the Iliad* is full of examples of men harming women, animals, and nature, the connection between Thetis and Achilles is always significant, he turns to his mother for help, all the time, yet he does not choose to respect nature she represents, the fact that Thetis is only seen as a part of Achilles' story and as the most woeful of mothers/immortals (Homer) reveal the biased attitude towards nature, and the marginalised other(s) in general, as criticized by ecofeminists. Duffy in "Thetis" builds upon this ecofeminist criticism and talks about how Thetis, as a representative of the Mother Goddess cult, takes different shapes through the ages only to be victimized, abused, and destroyed by the Anthropocene or androcentric practices. As a sea goddess and a mother goddess she stands for nature, women, nonhuman animals, and our planet in this poem. Several ecofeminists carefully reject the idea of Mother Earth, or the Mother Goddess cult because they suggest that some of these attempts pick a certain idea and detach it from its original context such as by abusing "the Native American conception of Mother Earth" (Gaard, "Ecofeminism and Native American Cultures" 301). Using the term "Mother Earth" out of its context, unfortunately, helps the domination of the marginalised others by the privileged culture which imposes patriarchal notions unto the bonds between women and nature. Duffy tries to reveal this problematic connection in "Thetis" as she shows her reader how Thetis falls victim to the destructive forces of the patriarchal culture in each shape she takes, from a small bird to a snake, from a fish to a flame ("Thetis" 231–2). The poem starts with the following lines from the mouth of the speaker:

> I shrank myself
> to the size of a bird in the hand
> of a man.
> Sweet, sweet, was the small song

that I sang,
till I felt the squeeze of his fist. (231)

This first stanza not only points out shapeshifting and the ability to find a new dwelling place in another being of nature, but it also underlines the different forms of androcentric destruction, *he* silences the bird's song and kills it in his fist. Then, Thetis takes the form of an albatross, which is a direct reference to Samuel Taylor Coleridge's albatross in "The Rime of the Ancyent Marinere". Coleridge stands as a unique poet within the Romantic tradition, because he can be seen as one of the few poets who come closer to talking about animal ethics in that period. In "The Rime of the Ancyent Marinere", the "friendship" of the albatross, and the curse that befalls on the mariner and his crew after he kills the bird (53) can be read as a criticism of animal cruelty. However, his poem's speaker is still the mariner, whereas Duffy chooses to look at the story from the albatross' eyes. Thetis, as the albatross, follows a ship only to feel *its* "wings/clipped by the squint of a crossbow's eye" (231), a crossbow that takes away first the freedom, and then the life out of the bird. This bird's-eye-view retelling of the story, in a few lines, not only pays homage to Derrida's idea of being seen by an animal, but also deconstructs the man's central position as the bird only mentions the ship, and the crossbow's eye but not the man behind it.

Each attempt of her, each shape she takes faces a similar, tragic end. Even when she takes the shape of a racoon, mink or a rat, she falls victim to a "taxidermist" (232), thus Duffy, in a way criticizes how achievements in science also mean further abuse of nature and nonhuman animals, as it is also used to experiment on them, or to turn them into collector's items. When she is the wind "a fighter plane" roars against her storm, and when her "tongue was flame" she is fought back with "asbestos" (232), so although she takes the form of natural beings, androcentric attitude fights back with human-related or human-made violent acts or weapons to destroy her existence.

The change comes when the speaker of the poem, the goddess, gives birth to a baby, she says "I changed, I learned" (232); as Dowson suggests "It is difficult not to find a feminist lens on her story of how she would dance to the tune of a man but then 'learn' that it brings abuse, domination, disappointment, and rejection. Moreover, it is in having the prophesied child and becoming a mother that Thetis is fulfilled" (139). However, it is essential to see that, more than the idea of a fulfillment, there is the connection between motherhood as another shape or a role a woman (or nature in this context) takes, and shrinking oneself to fit that shape only to be abused. There is also the dominant idea that a woman's body is also a dwelling place not only for herself but also for "housing" the baby, and it can be read as a symbol for the Western patriarchal outlook that chooses to see woman and nature as mother figures which they can use and abuse. For "In white Western culture, mothers are expected to be selfless, generous, and nurturing", so this bond, when taken up by the Western civilization what follows is the creation of a "connection between all-giving human mothers and the idea of nature as an all-giving mother" through which "the metaphor of Mother Earth will only serve to perpetuate the very notion ecofeminism seeks to eradicate" (Gaard, "Ecofeminism and Native American Cultures" 302).

Throughout "Thetis", Duffy shows the way anthropocentric or androcentric outlook fights with nature and all the marginalised others, and exhibits how the tools of destruction change drastically and get more violent. As Carol J. Adams and Lori Gruen suggest, ecofeminism "addresses the various ways that sexism, heteronormativity, racism, colonialism, and ableism are informed by and support speciesism and how analyzing the ways these forces intersect can produce less violent, more just practices" (1). Thus, the poem explicates the shape the Earth takes with this history of human destruction; therefore, it can also be suggested that through her critical approach to Mother Earth/Mother Goddess cult in "Thetis" Duffy also deals with the body, nature and our planet as a home, as a dwelling place. She not only critically rewrites the Mother Goddess cult by revealing the problems that surround a patriarchal approach but also explores the problems concerning the human approach to nature as humanity's first and primary dwelling-place; thus, in her poems, her ecofeminist approach is united with ecopoetics.

Following the current Covid-19 crisis which has stricken all humanity and pushed human civilization to reconsider its relationship with nature and the idea of home, Duffy "has launched an international poetry project with major names [...] as a response to the coronavirus pandemic" and she "leads British poets creating 'living record' of coronavirus" (Flood). Duffy, who believes in the exigency of poetry as a response to such dark moments, inevitably places particular importance on giving voice to the problematic relationship between nature and human civilization in her poetry. With its focus on the marginalised ones, the unique representation of nature, human and nonhuman others, and with the way she explores the possibilities and limits of language, Duffy's poetry is a significant example of ecofeminist ecopoetics.

"Ecological feminists ("ecofeminists") claim that there are important connections between the unjustified dominations of women, people of color, children, and the poor and the unjustified domination of nature" (Warren 1) and ecopoetics "asks in what respects a poem may be a making (Greek poiesis) of the dwelling-place" (Bate 75), Duffy's poetry unites both of them by critically investigating the dwelling places of human and nonhuman others: cities, villages and even bodies, history and literature as a dwelling place, and by giving voice to the dominated, marginalised women, people of color, nonhuman animals.

Ecopoetics is also a "healing process [which] requires a 'letting-be of Being' that allows for a rediscovery of familiarity with nature in which the idea of 'dwelling', immanently 'revealed' rather than instrumentally 'narrated'" (Huggan & Tiffin 106–7). Although Duffy's poems, specifically the ones discussed in this chapter, seem to draw a bleak picture of humanity as out of touch with nature, they create hope as Duffy tries to find ways to heal the wound of, therefore the trauma of, being out of touch with nature by exploring and proving the power of language and the way we use it, and creates a new dwelling-place, a new connection with our home (eco-) on a metaphorical, textual, and physical level.

Works Cited

Adams, Carol J. *The Sexual Politics of Meat: A Feminist-Vegetarian Critical Theory*. Continuum, 2010.

Adams, C. J., and Lori Gruen. "Introduction." *Ecofeminism: Feminist Intersections with Other Animals and the Earth*, edited by Carol J. Adams and Lori Gruen. Bloomsbury, 2014, pp. 1–6.

Aristotle. *Aristotle's History of Animals: In Ten Books,* translated by Richard Cresswell, Henry G. Bohn. Google Books, 1862. https://

books.google.com.tr/books?id=X7pfAAAAMAAJ&printsec=frontcove
r&hl=tr&source=gbs_ge_summary_r&cad=0#v=onepage&q&f=false

Bate, Jonathan. *The Song of the Earth*. Picador, 2000.

Berger, John. "Why Look at Animals?" *About Looking*. Vintage Books, 1991, pp. 3–28.

Birkeland, Janis. "Ecofeminism: Linking Theory and Practice." *Ecofeminism: Women, Animals, Nature*, edited by Greta Gaard. Temple University Press, 1993, pp. 13–59.

Coleridge, Samuel Taylor. "The Rime of the Ancyent Marinere." *Lyrical Ballads: 1798 and 1800,* William Wordsworth and Samuel Taylor Coleridge, edited by Michael Gamer and Dahlia Porter. Broadview Press, 2008.

Derrida, Jacques. *The Animal That Therefore I Am*. Edited by Marie-Louise Mallet, translated by David Wills. Fordham University Press, 2008.

Descartes, René. "Animals Are Machines." *Animal Rights and Human Obligations*, edited by Tom Regan and Peter Singer. Prentice Hall, 1989, pp. 13–19.

Dowson, Jane. *Carol Ann Duffy: Poet for Our Times*. Palgrave Macmillan, 2016.

Duffy, Carol Ann. "A Healthy Meal." *Collected Poems*. Picador, 2015a, p. 61.

Duffy, Carol Ann. "Model Village." *Collected Poems*. Picador, 2015b, pp. 79–81.

Duffy, Carol Ann. "Selling Manhattan." *Collected Poems*. Picador, 2015c, pp. 94–5.

Duffy, Carol Ann. "The Dolphins." *Collected Poems*. Picador, 2015d, p. 59.

Duffy, Carol Ann. "The English Elms." *Collected Poems*. Picador, 2015e, pp. 467–8.

Duffy, Carol Ann. "Thetis." *Collected Poems*. Picador, 2015f, pp. 231–2.

Duffy, Carol Ann. "Into thin air: Carol Ann Duffy presents poems about our vanishing insect world." *The Guardian* [London], 27 April 2019.

Flood, Alison. "Carol Ann Duffy leads British poets creating 'living record' of coronavirus." *The Guardian* [London], 21 April 2020.

Forbes, Peter. "Winning lines." *The Guardian* [London],
31 August 2002.

Gaard, Greta. "Ecofeminism and Native American Cultures: Pushing
the Limits of Cultural Imperialism?" *Ecofeminism: Women, Animals,
Nature*, edited by Greta Gaard. Temple University Press, 1993a,
pp. 295–314.

Gaard, Greta. "Living Interconnections with Animals and Nature."
Ecofeminism: Women, Animals, Nature, edited by Greta Gaard.
Temple University Press, 1993b, pp. 1–12.

Gaard, Greta. "Vegetarian Ecofeminism: A Review Essay." *Frontiers: A
Journal of Women Studies*, Vol. 23, No. 3, 2002, pp. 117–146. *Project
Muse*, https://doi.org/10.1353/fro.2003.0006.

Garrard, Greg. *Ecocriticism*. Routledge, 2012.

George, Andrew, translator. *The Epic of Gilgamesh*. Penguin
Books, 2003.

Gifford, Terry. *Green Voices: Understanding Contemporary Nature
Poetry*. Manchester University Press, 1995.

Homer. *The Iliad,* translated by Anthony Verity. Oxford University
Press, 2012.

Huggan, Graham, and Helen Tiffin. *Postcolonial Ecocriticism: Literature,
Animals, Environment*. Routledge, 2010.

Kant, Immanuel. "Duties to Animals and Spirits." *Lectures on Ethics*,
translated by Louis Infield. Harper and Row, 1963, pp. 239–41.

Lefebvre, Henri. Writing on Cities, translated and edited by Eleonore
Kofman and Elizabeth Lebas. Blackwell Publishing, 2008.

Mies, Maria. "White Man's Dilemma: His Search for What He Has
Destroyed." *Ecofeminism*, Maria Mies & Vandana Shiva. Zed Books,
1993, pp. 132–163.

Moe, Aaron M. *Zoopoetics: Animals and the Making of Poetry*.
Lexington Books, 2014.

Nolan, Sarah. *Unnatural Ecopoetics: Unlikely Spaces in Contemporary
Poetry*. University of Nevada Press, 2017, Google Books, https://
books.google.com.tr/books?id=fCuVDwAAQBAJ&dq=sarah%20
nolan%2C&hl=tr&source=gbs_book_other_versions.

"Pastor." *Oxford Concise Dictionary of English Etymology,* edited by T. F. Hoad. Oxford University Press, 2000, p. 339.

Skinner, Jonathan. "Editor's Statement." *ecopoetics,* edited by Jonathan Skinner, vol. 1, Winter 2001, pp. 5–8.

Warren, Karen J. *Ecofeminist Philosophy: A Western Perspective on What It Is and Why It Matters.* Rowman & Littlefield Publishers, 2000.

White, Jr., Lynn. "Historical Roots of Our Ecologic Crisis." *The Ecocriticism Reader: Landmarks in Literary Ecology,* edited by Cheryll Glotfelty and Harold Fromm. The University of Georgia Press, 1996, pp. 3–14.

Winterson, Jeanette. "On the Poetry of Carol Ann Duffy—Of Course It's Political." *The Guardian,* 17 January 2015.

Winterson, Jeanette. "Can You Move Diagonally? Interview with the Poet Laureate, Carol Ann Duffy." *The Times,* 29 August 2009.

Notes on the Contributors

Editors: Özden Sözalan and İnci Bilgin Tekin

Contributors:

Burcu Kayışcı Akkoyun (Ph.D.) completed her Ph.D. in Literary Studies at Monash University in 2015 with a dissertation on the literary representations of the end entitled "Imagining the End: Comic Perspectives and Critical Spaces." Her fields of interest are utopian and dystopian fiction, ecocriticism, identity politics, and narrative theory. She currently teaches in the Department of Western Languages and Literatures at Boğaziçi University.

Ayşe Beyza Artukaslan (MA) holds a bachelor degree from American Culture and Literature department at Istanbul University, and a master's degree from English Language and Literature department at Bogazici University. She is now a research assistant at Istanbul Sehir University and a literary translator. Her research areas are ecocrititism, ecopoetry, animal studies, modern and contemporary poetry.

Ferdi Çetin (Ph.D.) studied American Culture and Literature at Istanbul University, and obtained his Ph.D. in theater studies at the same university with a dissertation on Heiner Goebbels. He also works as a dramaturg and project director at GalataPerform and he has been working with emerging playwrights in New Text New Theater Project, for which he has also translated several plays. His stories have appeared in different magazines and his first short story collection titled *this is how I burnt our house* was published by YKY Publishing House in 2019. In 2012 he founded *ba- interdisciplinary art ensemble* with Yusuf Demirkol and he has been writing performance texts for the ensemble including *Letters for a Tractor from The Museum with a Memory Loss* (2016).

Özlem Karadağ (Ph.D.) teaches in the English Department at Istanbul University, specializing in theater studies, trauma narratives, and ecocriticism. She received her BA (2005), MA (2008), and Ph.D. (2013) degrees from Istanbul University's English Language and Literature

Department and took a postdoctoral position at Queen Mary University of London, Department of Drama (2015), where she had also conducted her Ph.D. research in 2012. In 2012, she joined BuluTiyatro as a resident dramaturg and has also translated many contemporary English plays, which have gone on to be produced by theater companies in Istanbul. She is one of the editors of a forthcoming anthology of Turkish drama to be published by Laertes of Chapel Hill.

Nilay Kaya (Ph.D.) teaches in the Department of Comparative Literature at Istanbul Bilgi University. Her doctoral studies in Ankara, Bilkent University, was focused on Evliyâ Çelebi's *Seyahatnâme* (The Book of Travels). She was a visiting scholar in Università Ca' Foscari Venezia's Department of Asian and North African Studies in 2018–2019, conducting a research on 17th-century Venetian travelogues about Ottoman world. Her academic interests are travelogues, visuality and literature, modern Turkish literature and Brontë studies. Beside her academic studies, she translates Children's & Young Adult Books and writes reviews on them.

Ekin Gündüz Özdemirci (Ph.D.) currently works in Environmental Humanities Centre at Cappadocia University and teaches in graduate programs. Her main research interest has been the question of filmic representations, particularly related to environmental studies and ecocriticism. She pursued her work on the analysis of ecological representations in Turkish films during her fellowship at the Rachel Carson Centre for Environment and Society, LMU between 2017 and 2018. Between 2014 and 2015 she was a visiting scholar at the Brunel University where she conducted research on environmental sustainability in the British film industry. Besides her academic research, she is involved in civil society works on art and ecology, participated in the Applied Ecovillage Living Training in Findhorn Ecovillage, gained a permaculture design certificate, visited ecological communities, sustainable living centers and did voluntary work there.

Canan Şavkay (Ph.D.) After completing her studies at Albert-Ludwigs-University, Freiburg, Germany with an M.A. degree in English Literature, Canan Şavkay moved to Istanbul where she continued her postgraduate studies at Istanbul University, Department of English Language and

Literature. She currently works as Associate Professor in the same department. Her research fields include ethics, ecocriticism and gender studies.

Özden Sözalan (Ph.D. Essex, 2000) is professor of literature and head of English department at İstanbul Bilgi University. She has published books and journal articles on contemporary theories of literature and theater. Her recent research interest involves environmental literature and posthumanist theory.

İnci Bilgin Tekin (Ph.D.) teaches in the English Department at İstanbul Bilgi University. Bilgin Tekin is the author of two books, *Myths of Oppression Revisited in Liz Lochhead and Cherrie Moraga's Plays* (Ibidem, Columbia UP, 2012) and *Female Othellos* (Peter Lang, 2018) as well as several articles. Her research interest broadly involves adaptation and reception studies, postcolonial and feminist theories, Shakespearean studies and contemporary literature.

Zeynep Talay Turner (Ph.D.) She did her Ph.D. in Philosophy at the Polish Academy of Sciences, Warsaw (2013), after she had completed her MA in Philosophy at Warwick University, U.K. (2007). She currently teaches philosophy at İstanbul Bilgi University. Her research interests lie in the area of Philosophy and Literature, Ethics, 19th and 20th Century Continental Philosophy, Philosophies of the Self. She is the author of *Philosophy, Literature and the Dissolution of the Subject* (Peter Lang, 2014) and numerous articles on related subjects.

Sinem Yazıcıoğlu (Ph.D.) teaches in the Department of American Culture and Literature at Istanbul University. Her teaching focuses on literary theory, cultural studies, the American short story and Canadian literature. In her published essays, she analyzes literary texts within a spatial framework and explores the broader theoretical discussions in urban studies, trauma studies, geocriticism, postmodernism and commodification. Her research interests concentrate on literary dystopias and heterotopias, the urban space in literature and American westward expansion.